BRITISH RAILWAYS ILLUSTRATED

Annual Number 11

Welcome to British Railways Illu

Eleventy Years Old!

Grow Old Gracefully with Irwell Press - Welcome to British Railways Illustrated Annual No.11. All New Photographs and Articles!

Frontispiece. An Eric Treacy print of 46252 CITY OF LEICESTER approaching Beattock Summit with a Birmingham-Glasgow train. A classic shot by the Master.

Cover photograph. The year A4s came to New England, 1963. B. Richardson, The Transport Treasury.

Rear cover. 5072 HURRICANE prepared to work the 7.20pm 'Crewe Mail' as far as Shrewsbury, on 21 April 1956. In the background is a WD ready to take out an eastbound goods or mineral along with 7020 GLOUCESTER CASTLE. R.O. Tuck.

EDITORIAL MATTERS
Contributions, submissions, photographs or whatever (remember the contributor must address and attend to copyright), readers' letters, bouquets and brickbats for British Railways Illustrated must be addressed to Editor,
Chris Hawkins
at 59A, High Street, Clophill, Bedfordshire MK45 4BE
E-mail chris@irwellpress.co.uk
Tel.01525 861888 or
Fax. 01525 862044
Printed & Bound by
Newton Printing Ltd, London W1
www.newtonprinting.com

Through The Years At Brighton Shed

By Bryan Wilson

In 1913, the engine shed at Brighton was 158 feet long and 201 feet wide with fourteen roads. Between this building and the main running lines was a separate shed 483 feet long with three roads. This had been built as a four road carriage shed and later became Brighton Works stock shed, one road having been removed. Later still it became a 'running' shed. It was equipped for 'washouts' and had the unusual feature of connections between the lines within the building. In the 1920s, it was known as the 'new' shed and used to prepare locomotives for their duties. Unlike the larger shed, it had access at the station end and an exit at the north end. On electrification in the 1930s, this 'new' shed was abandoned for locomotive work and was subsequently used for motor vehicle maintenance, until 1964. There was also an engine siding and 60ft turntable, dating from 1910, between the Main and 'East' lines at Montpelier Junction.

The track layout in Brighton station approaches did not lend itself to through working between East and West lines. Only Platform 3 had access to the Main line and to both coastal routes. In 1925, Brighton had an allocation of 124 locomotives. This was greatly reduced with the electrification of the lines from Three Bridges to Hove and Worthing from 1 January 1933 followed by Keymer Junction to Lewes and Ore on 7 July 1935, together with Brighton-Lewes. The West Coast route from the limit of the 1932 electrification at West Worthing to Havant, plus the Mid Sussex line via Horsham and Arundel followed in July 1938.

Brighton is usually thought of as an 'Electric' stronghold in post-World War II days. Whilst there was indeed a strong electric presence after the 1930s electrification schemes, there was still plenty of steam interest remaining. In fact, between 1949 and the closure of Brighton shed to steam on 15 June 1964, no less than 37 different classes of steam locomotive were allocated to 75A at some time or other. Add to this the 'visitors' which inevitably came to this seaside resort plus locos attending or built at the local Workshops and we have a heady mix to survey.

If all this were not enough to make it interesting, Brighton for some reason did not seem to get on well with its Pacific allocation. Day after day, locomotives of lesser power were substituted to their duties. Smart they may have looked but in 1952 the average mileage for Brighton West Countries stood at 19,618. Compare this with Bournemouth at 34,000 and a hefty 51,000 for Ramsgate. So it couldn't be the seaside that was the problem. And why, one may ask, with the Works that built them close by and the relevant expertise that went with it, plus presumably a better supply of 'spares' available than to say, Plymouth Friary, didn't they do better? And how was it that when Atlantics had covered the Bournemouth job all week, there

The curving, narrowing Platform 1 and 2, for the services west along the coast, allowed observers almost into the shed yard itself. 34086 219 SQUADRON rumbles along to get to the shed; the date is not known but given the AWS battery box at the front and the electrification flashes, it is about 1962. 34086 was an Exmouth Junction engine so has probably come off a Plymouth-Brighton service. Photograph The Transport Treasury.

was a healthy West Country to take a Special to Wembley on a Saturday?

Brighton was a place which had no qualms in providing 2-6-4Ts on Pacific jobs to Salisbury, Bournemouth or London and even a 2-6-2T to London occasionally if needs must. Many of the passenger jobs were relatively short distance, occasioned by the fact that trains reversed frequently. For instance, the Birkenhead-Brighton trains reversed at Redhill and if going on to Eastbourne and Hastings, reversed twice more making for many engine changes. Such trips could fall equally to a K 2-6-0, a Schools or even to an E4 radial tank of which Brighton housed 38 different members (with a maximum of sixteen on the books at any one time) during the period under review. Having 'set the scene', we will look at the Engines, the Men, and take a glance through the years from 1947 until the end of steam.

This article deals only with the steam workings for engines and men from Brighton shed. It does not cover 'Motormen' or multiple unit workings, neither does it cover the separate subject of Brighton Locomotive Works, although of course shunting work was carried out there and '75A' ran-in both new and repaired locomotives released from the CM & EE's Department.

We would do well indeed to recall H. Holcroft's comment in his book 'Locomotive Adventure' that 'Only running lines and a few sidings separated Works and adjacent running sheds but they might as well have been 50 miles apart.' That comment may help to explain the 'Pacific problems' and some of the 'matters arising' as we pass through the years at Brighton. At the beginning of 1947, Brighton housed 71 locomotives. These comprised:-

P 0-6-0T: 1178, 1557
E1 0-6-0T: 2122, 2127, 2153, 2606
D1 0-4-2T: 2235
D3 0-4-4T: 2368, 2372, 2376, 2385, 2386, 2397
E4 0-6-2T: 2470, 2471, 2480, 2486, 2491, 2496, 2505, 2513, 2566
E5 0-6-2T: 2567, 2583, 2587, 2592
E5X 0-6-2T: 2576
I3 4-4-2T: 2079, 2080, 2084, 2086, 2088
H1 4-4-2: 2037, 2038, 2039
C2X 0-6-0: 2437, 2438, 2443, 2523, 2528, 2539, 2543, 2546
L12 4-4-0: 423, 428, 430

Glorious steam and shadow wreathed around one of Brighton's E4 0-6-2T stalwarts, 32503, early in the 1960s. A long-standing Tonbridge engine, it came to Brighton in September 1955. This little gem was still working to Horsham and Guildford in mid-1962 and was finally withdrawn in April 1963. Photograph The Transport Treasury.

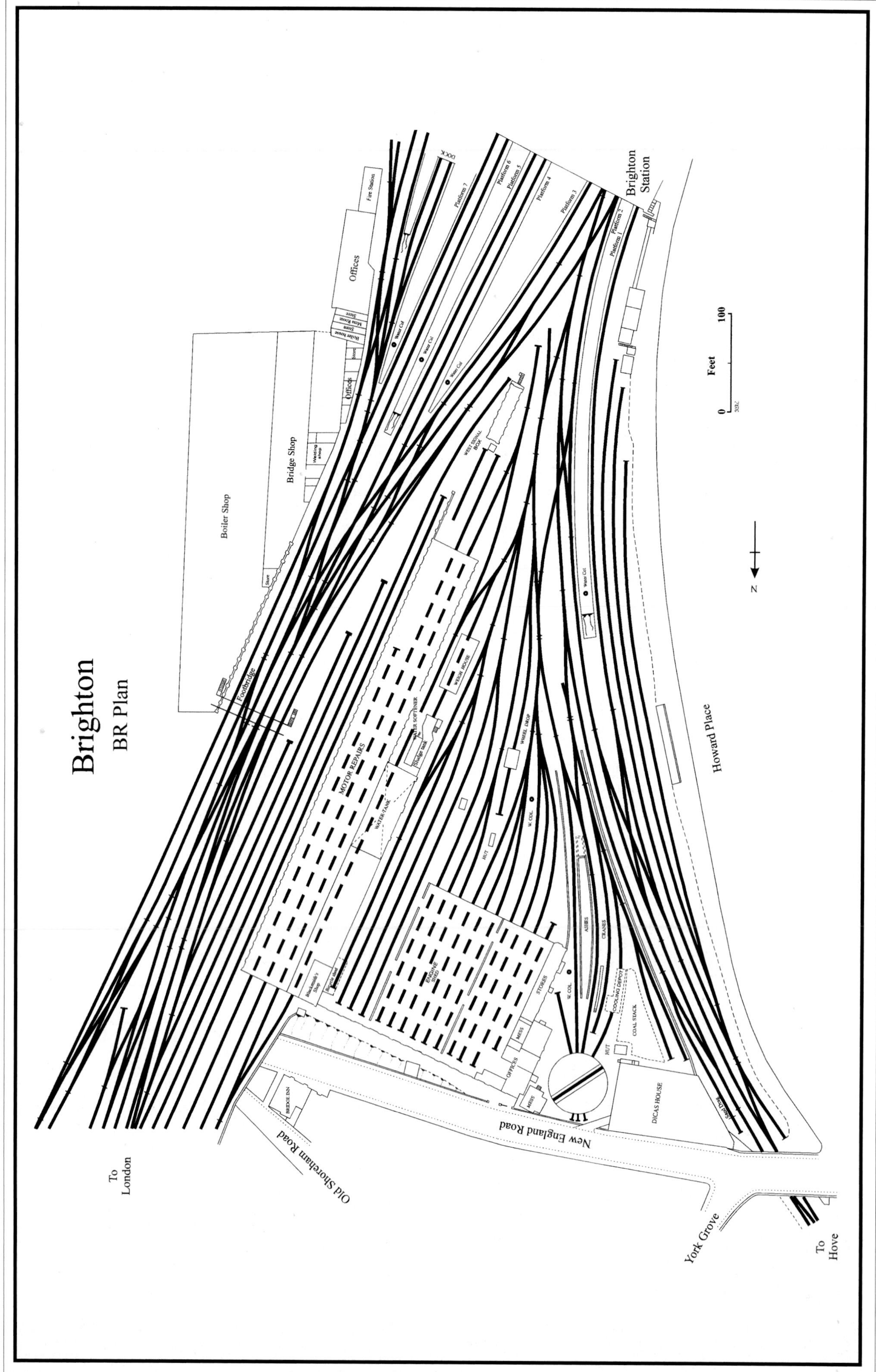
Brighton
BR Plan
To London
To Hove
Brighton Station
Platform 1
Platform 2
Platform 3
Platform 4
Platform 5
Platform 6
Platform 7
Fire Station
Offices
Boiler Shop
Bridge Shop
Footbridge
MOTOR REPAIRS
WATER SOFTENER
WATER TANK
WEIGH HOUSE
WEST SIGNAL BOX
WHEEL DROP
ENGINE SHED
STORES
MESS
OFFICES
ASHES
CRANES
COAL STACK
HUT
DICAS HOUSE
BRIDGE INN
New England Road
Old Shoreham Road
York Grove
Howard Place
Feet
0
100
N

That wonderful vista off the end of Platforms 1/2. Given its setting, all trains out of Brighton went 'north', out of the station. Most engines are thus stabled 'pointing out', that is, tenders/bunkers to the 'south'. Photograph The Transport Treasury.

V 4-4-0: 928, 929, 930
B4X 4-4-0: 2043, 2052, 2071, 2072, 2073
N 2-6-0: 1406, 1817, 1843, 1851, 1854, 1858
K 2-6-0: 2337, 2338, 2339, 2340, 2341, 2342, 2343, 2344, 2345, 2346, 2347

The three 'Schools' arrived in November 1946 as the Netley line had been cleared for their use and a restricted bridge at Ford rebuilt. They replaced L12s 423, 428 and 430 which passed to Eastleigh in June 1947. L12s had been on the 'West' workings from mid-1925 until mid-1940 and returned again in October 1945. The 'Schools' hardly settled in when the 1947 fuel cuts resulted in the cancellation of the trains they worked. 928 and 929, having been kept for the summer, went to 'The Brick' in September 1947, followed by 930 in December.

In 1947, the H1 Atlantics were still on London turns. This was in place of B4Xs and they covered Newhaven turns as necessary. 2038, outstationed at Newhaven, was on a Brighton-Birkenhead working as far as Redhill in May 1949.

In July 1947 the six Ns went to Redhill, replaced by U1s. A brief summary of the work performed during the summer of 1947 would look like this:

Schools for the Saturday only Bournemouth job.

K/B4X for van trains to London Bridge, New Cross etc.

D3 Push & Pull for the Horsham line plus the odd trip to Sheffield Park and Horsted Keynes.

Ks for the heavy freight work at the coastal end of the LB&SC with freights to Bricklayers Arms, Norwood, Portsmouth and Hastings.

E4 Radial Tanks for short distance passengers (portions of through trains to Eastbourne and so on) and the 'Lancing Belle' Workmen's trains.

0-6-0Ts of the P class shunted Kingston Wharf at Shoreham due to the severe curvature in the sidings. They replaced the shunting horse there in 1938 when an incline with a winding engine was replaced by a realigned siding connecting Yard and Quayside. A1Xs were prohibited due to their tendency to buffer lock with vehicles and any shortfall in the P Class was covered by 'borrowed' B4 0-4-0Ts. The Ps also occasionally covered the Loco coal shunt.

At the end of 1947, Brighton took its share of the WD 2-8-0s on offer when 77007, 77270, 77286 and 77340 arrived releasing a couple of K 2-6-0s to Fratton. These big engines were not really suited to SR work and all left in 1950 (as 90107, 90347, 90354 and 90247 respectively) plus 90345 which was on the books from June 1949 to September 1950. When they went, three Ks came back. Modernisation also came to the area, in the shape of the Bulleid/Raworth Co-Cos 20001 and 20003 working the 9.41 Lovers Walk to Redhill Vans from Preston Park (Lovers Walk sidings were not electrified).

Another sign of things to come was LM 2-6-4T 42199 on trials to Victoria via Eridge and Uckfield on Tunbridge Wells 663 Turn during 4-16 June 1948. Nine of these locos arrived new between March and June 1951 and 'saw off' the I1X, I3, J1 and J2 passenger tanks. Individual LM-type tanks came and went but seven were still on the books until 1956 when five were replaced by the more popular BR engines, 80145-54.

New West Countrys were 'running in' from Brighton Works, usually on the 9.41am Brighton-Redhill vans although none was allocated to Brighton until the autumn of 1948 when 21C133, 34034 and 34035 arrived. 34034 worked down to Brighton with the 4.50pm from Victoria via Eridge on 28 September; this was the first to work to Brighton in normal service, though there had been trials in 1945 with 21C101 and 21C103. 21C155 had been named FIGHTER PILOT at Brighton on 19 September 1947 but it was another 12½ years before it was allocated there. When the Pacifics came, the B4Xs went to store at Eastbourne and Redhill.

The year 1948 saw the reinstatement of the daily trains to Bournemouth, Cardiff and Plymouth (the latter two worked by Brighton as far as Salisbury) and the Pacifics should have made light of this. As often happened, the initial batch did not stay, being replaced in December by 34037-34040 – the Southern certainly seemed to like doing things in batches.

The summer of 1949 saw both Ks and H2 Atlantics on the cross-country services between Brighton and Eastbourne, Brighton to Redhill (with the Birkenhead) and to Willesden. Schools from other sheds were already replacing ailing Pacifics on the Bournemouth job. The Bulleids by now were also allocated to the 11.18pm Vans to London Bridge, returning with the 3.25am News.

The popular Atlantics were substituting for the 4-6-2s on both Bournemouth and Plymouth services (the latter to Salisbury) in the spring of 1950, at a time when there were seven Pacifics (34035-34041 inclusive) on the allocation for four jobs and yet, 34040 worked a Special to Wembley on 15 April!

That summer of 1950 again saw 32422 and 32424 on the Hastings-Birmingham between Brighton and Redhill and working to Bournemouth. At the end of June, B4X 32072 of Eastbourne was on the Bournemouth covering the locomotives meant to replace it! The Ks had a busy summer with the Austerities going and the additional Saturday jobs to cover but, as always, they were extremely competent at their task, although never easy with the faster passenger work.

The shortage of Pacifics continued in August, the 6.58am Brighton-Oxted-London Bridge going two months without one but, you've guessed it, come the autumn 34039 and 34040 went to Wembley and 34037 to Kensington with Excursions. At the end of 1950, however, Pacifics were (hopefully) shown to cover the 6.0pm Brighton-London Bridge vans and 10.40 return, plus the 12.30am Freight to Bricklayers Arms and 5.31am return 'Fish' from London Bridge. In reality, a U1 tended to cover the latter working.

Fuel economies struck again early in 1951 and produced some strange results. In mid-January, the through services to the West were again cancelled and one of the 'hard to find' Pacifics found itself on the 10.18am Brighton-Victoria via Eridge and 3.52pm return, in place of a U1. Likewise, on 27 January, 34036 was working in place of a K 2-6-0. With the lack of suitable work during the crisis, 34037 and 34038 went to Plymouth Friary, 34039 to Stratford and 34040 and 34041 to Bath during May. When services resumed in June, it was four different locos that came to 75A. This time it was 34045, 34046, 34047 and 34048 from Salisbury and these, together with 34039 when it returned from Stratford in March 1952, struggled to cover their allocated work for the next seven years.

A further taste of 'things to come' was LM 2-6-2T 41297 of Three Bridges working into Brighton in November. Six months later 41313, 41314 and 41315 arrived but only stayed a month before moving to the West of England. It was January 1961 before the class returned to replace the H 0-4-4Ts on the Horsham line. The end of 1951 is time to 'take stock'; 75A's allocation at 1 January 1952 was 48 locomotives:

WC 4-6-2: 34045, 34046, 34047, 34048
H2 4-4-2: 32422, 32426
C2X 0-6-0: 32438, 32442, 32523, 32543
K 2-6-0: 32337, 32338, 32339, 32340, 32341, 32342, 32343, 32344, 32347
D3 0-4-4T: 32365, 32368, 32372, 32376
P 0-6-0T: 31325, 31556
U1 2-6-0: 31894, 31896
E3 0-6-2T: 32168, 32170
E4 0-6-2T: 32471, 32486, 32508, 32513, 32514, 32566, 32577
E5 0-6-2T: 32573, 32583
E5X 0-6-2T: 32576
LM 2-6-4T: 42085, 42086, 42087, 42088, 42089, 42090, 42091, 42092, 42093

December 1951 saw the BR Standard Class 4 2-6-4Ts 'running-in' and in January 1952 80017, 80018 and 80019 arrived from Tunbridge Wells. They were replaced by 80031, 80032 and 80033 in March. By 1956 there were fifteen of these popular locos on the books. They had replaced the majority of the LM 2-6-4Ts and three of the H2s (32421, 32425 and 32426). The Standard tanks worked mainly on the Tunbridge Wells, Tonbridge and Redhill routes but also had turns to Beeding, Shoreham and Hove with freights. They worked to Victoria via Oxted, to Norwood and Bricklayers Arms and even had a

Motor fitted M7 0-4-4T 30056 declaring 'no fixed abode' on the smokebox door, outside the shed on 12 January 1957. This was the first of its three spells at Brighton between May 1956 and April 1961. Being 'LSW' they were not popular with the Brighton men. Photograph Frank Hornby.

turn as Forest Hill banker in South London during a 'layover'. They also worked to East Grinstead, Eastbourne and Haywards Heath, particularly with van trains.

In later years the BR 2-6-4Ts were renowned for their 'lodging'. On a normal night, one was at Norwood, one at Eastbourne and four at Tunbridge Wells West (though no Tunbridge Wells loco normally worked to Brighton). As already mentioned, they capably covered the Bournemouth job when necessary and covered odd turns on the Horsham branch via Steyning. Between February 1961 and July 1963 there were seventeen of the 2-6-4Ts at Brighton and the last seven went with the shed's closure in June 1964.

Top and above. Brighton was one of the most perfectly 'visible' sheds there were. not only did the long platform at the station give access almost into the heart of the shed yard, a brisk walk up the nearby hill of Howard Place brought a view barely rivalled elsewhere (though Worcester comes to mind). These two wonderful overviews, with a splendid array of Southern steam, were taken on 14 May 1958. The Atlantic 32424 BEACHY HEAD had just done its last RCTS run and was due for withdrawal. The raincoats flap wilder and wider as the cognoscenti snaffle up Terriers, an S15 30506, Pacifics, E4 0-6-2Ts, K and U Moguls, C2X 0-6-0s, M7s, BR tanks and who can guess at what else. There are few more marvellous sights than these. Photographs Frank Hornby.

Brighton Allocation as at 31 December 1949-1963

Year	'49	'50	'51	'52	'53	'54	'55	'56	'57	'58	'59	'60	'61	'62	'63	CLASS
WC/BB	4	5	4	5	5	5	5	5	5	5	5	5	5	10	-	WC/BD
V	-	-	-	-	-	-	-	-	-	2	6	6	7	-	-	V
H1	1	1	-	-	-	-	-	-	-	-	-	-	-	-	-	H1
H2	3	2	2	3	3	3	3	1	1	-	-	-	-	-	-	H2
BR4 4-6-0	-	-	-	-	-	-	-	-	-	-	1	-	-	-	-	BR4 4-6-0
BR4 2-6-0	-	-	-	-	-	-	-	-	-	-	-	-	-	5	-	BR4 2-6-0
L	-	-	-	-	-	-	-	3	3	3	-	-	-	-	-	L
N	-	-	-	-	-	-	-	-	-	-	-	-	4	12	3	N
U1	6	5	2	2	2	6	-	-	-	-	2	2	-	4	-	U1
J1	-	1	-	-	-	-	-	-	-	-	-	-	-	-	-	J1
J2	-	1	-	-	-	-	-	-	-	-	-	-	-	-	-	J2
11X	-	3	-	-	-	-	-	-	-	-	-	-	-	-	-	11X
I3	4	1	-	-	-	-	-	-	-	-	-	-	-	-	-	I3
E3	1		2	5	4	4	-	-	-	-	-	-	-	-	-	E3
E4	10	9	7	8	8	9	16	16	16	15	10	9	6	4	-	E4
E5	5	5	2	5	3	-	-	-	-	-	-	-	-	-	-	E5
E5X	1	1	1	2	2	1	1	-	-	-	-	-	-	-	-	E5X
E6	-	-	-	-	-	-	-	-	-	-	-	-	2	-	-	E6
M7	-	-	-	-	-	-	1	5	3	6	6	9	-	-	-	M7
D1	-	-	-	-	-	-	-	-	-	-	-	-	-	-	-	D1 (1 until Sep 49)
D3	5	5	4	3	1	1	-	-	-	-	-	-	-	-	-	D3
H	-	-	-	-	3	3	-	-	-	-	4	5	-	-	-	H
LM 2-6-2T	-	-	-	-	-	-	-	-	-	-	-	-	12	15	14	LM 2-6-2T
LM 2-6-4T	-	-	9	7	9	8	7	2	2	2	-	-	-	-	-	LM 2-6-4T
BR 2-6-2T	-	-	-	-	-	-	-	-	-	-	-	-	-	-	-	BR 2-6-2T (May-Sep 1961)
BR 2-6-4T	-	-	-	4	5	5	5	15	15	16	16	16	17	17	8	BR 2-6-4T
C	-	-	-	-	-	-	2	2	2	2	2	2	-	-	-	C
C2X	6	6	4	3	3	3	4	6	4	2	2	1	-	-	-	C2X
WD	4	-	-	-	-	-	-	-	-	-	-	-	-	-	-	WD
Q1	-	-	-	-	-	-	-	-	-	-	-	-	-	-	-	Q1 (May-Oct 1954)
K	5	10	9	8	8	6	6	6	6	6	6	8	8	-	-	K
700	-	-	-	-	-	-	-	-	-	-	-	-	2	-	-	700
Q	-	-	-	-	-	-	-	-	-	-	-	-	4	-	2	Q
E1	3	2	-	-	-	-	-	-	-	-	-	-	-	-	-	E1
Z	-	-	-	-	1	1	-	-	-	-	-	-	-	-	-	Z
A1X	-	-	-	-	-	-	4	2	2	3	4	4	4	4	-	A1X
P	2	2	2	2	2	3	2	2	1	2	2	1	-	-	-	P

But we are running ahead. Into 1952 the H2s were still active with 32422, 32424 and 32426 all working to London. The ever-popular K 2-6-0s now ventured as far as Reading South on 761 turn which ran 8.0am from Lewes to Merstham, 2.5pm Redhill to Reading and 7.20pm return. They also had the Leicester-Hastings passenger between Brighton and Eastbourne.

That summer, the long-established Newhaven main line turns were transferred to Brighton (with 32425) and Atlantics were covering the Kensington and Willesden jobs (733/734 turns) in place of West Countrys. Despite this, on 2 August 1952 34039 worked a Stoke-Brighton special from Willesden and 34046 worked locally from Brighton to Eastbourne. On this same date, all five H2s appeared at Willesden on express work... At the end of 1952 summer service, Eastbourne shed closed as any sort of independent unit. This, together with the partial closure of Polegate Yard and a revision of services and stabling resulted in E4/5s 32485, 32518, 32585 and 32588 moving into Brighton.

The autumn saw 32421 and 32426 monopolising the Bournemouth job, Standard 2-6-4Ts were working the Cardiff train to Salisbury (being more economical than the LM type). At the same time 34039 was well enough to work a Brighton-Yeovil football special through via Eastleigh and Salisbury on 22 November, while Atlantics and 2-6-4Ts, plus the odd T9, N and even a D15 covered the Pacific work.

The D3 0-4-4Ts were regulars on the Horsham branch but towards the end of 1952 one of them, 32368, appeared on the Sunday 5.52am Brighton-Seaford and 8.01 return while the electricity supply was isolated during engineering operations. This occurred again in March 1953. At the turn of the year, T9 30304 came home with the Bournemouth on 30 December covering 34046 which had failed there. The following week the same T9 was covering the failure of 34048.

The relatively unpopular Fairburn 2-6-4Ts now had an evening cement train turn from Shoreham to Southampton. This train originated at Beeding. By March 1953, Brighton had a shortage of 2-6-4Ts and 42075, 42077 and 42082 came in, but not before the three Atlantics had been taken out of store to cover the shortfall.

A big surprise (literally) was the arrival of Z Class 0-8-0T in April 1953 for work as the Lovers Walk Pilot which it covered until summer 1954. At one period during that particular month, none of the Pacifics was available. Atlantics and Standard tanks dug them out as usual and 80033 even worked from Willesden to Eastbourne with a special from Coventry on 8 August.

The September 1953 Timetable saw the D3 duties eliminated and only 32390, which had arrived from St Leonards in March, remained. It became the shed coal pilot. In their heyday they had worked the Kemp Town and Dyke Branches plus trips to East Grinstead. Meanwhile, 'officialdom' had recognised the Pacific position and the Bournemouth job was now booked for an H2 – whilst 34048 worked the Beeding-Southampton cement and 34046 managed a football trip to Southampton in November.

With the demise of the D3s, H Class 0-4-4Ts 31310, 31319 and 31320 took over their duties until June 1955 when the first M7 (30031) arrived. The Brighton-Horsham jobs also encompassed trips from Horsham to Guildford 'all in a day's work'. Having said all that, 32390 still managed trips to Guildford at the end of the year.

The first surprise of 1954 was BR Standard 4 2-6-0s coming 'on loan' to Brighton on 15/16 January. They worked the 8.20 and 11.02am Brighton-Victoria via Oxted. They were 'indifferent steamers' and were passed on to Dorchester in April. Meanwhile, 34039 and 34046 had reached an all time low, working coal trains between Polegate and Kingston Wharf via Haywards Heath in March while the Ks happily dealt with the football traffic to Hove. 34045 made a trip with a Newhaven boat train in April.

Another new class appeared in May when Q1s 33017 and 33037 arrived to deal with a heavy programme of engineering work in Balcombe Tunnel between Haywards Heath and Three Bridges. They stayed for five months. The 1954 summer saw 32424 and 32425

34086 219 SQUADRON, seen earlier, has run down to the turntable and coal/ash roads, down by the New England Road entrance (strange that access to Brighton came via a road named after another famous shed, which also had Atlantics in its day...); note the curious differences in the ground levels. 34086 is in good company with E4s 32479 on the coal shunt, 32503 just arrived and Terrier 32646 (of Fratton) as shed pilot. And, inside the shed, is that one of the Brighton West Countrys in the usual pose of 'Not To Be Moved'? Photograph The Transport Treasury.

working to Kensington and Clapham Junction with excursions. One particularly interesting one took 32425 from Clapham Junction to Portsmouth via Three Bridges, Horsham and the Mid Sussex Line.

The winter timetable and diagrams showed Pacifics working the 9.34pm freight Brighton-Norwood and 3.25am News London Bridge-Brighton, plus the 11.18pm vans to London Bridge and 5.32am return. With the 0-8-0T ending its spell at Lovers Walk during the summer and two more, 30955 and 30956 arriving from Eastleigh, all three were 'on shed' with no work in mid-August. There was not enough work, it seems, for locos that the shed had, but not enough locos of the right sort for the work Brighton did have. Only 30956 was still at the premises at the end of the year.

A blow was dealt to the Atlantics when a new Engine Restriction Booklet of 14 June 1954 banned them west of Farlington Junction thus depriving them of the Bournemouth job. 32422 and 32425 went to store at Newhaven on 26 October. E3s appeared on passenger work during the autumn with a shortage of 2-6-4Ts; Standard 2-6-0 76007 and Pacific 34070 were on loan in September.

The Horsham line had an interesting period being covered by E4 0-6-2Ts, the remaining D3, H 0-4-4Ts and Ivatt 2-6-2Ts. The last E5 on the books, 32583, transferred to Basingstoke on 19 November 1954. In December, U1s 31900, 31901, 31902 and 31903 moved in from Stewarts Lane. In the other direction, 42088 passed to Battersea. The 2-6-0s quickly took over the Brighton-London Bridge and Victoria services via Uckfield and East Grinstead.

The D3, 32390, after a period in store – almost everything had a period in store, it seems, at some time or other on the Southern – did further work to Horsham and as the station pilot. Atlantics 32422 and 32425 came back into action for the Christmas parcel traffic and they crept back onto the Birkenhead passenger as far as Redhill. The West Coast services soldiered on with a mixture of U1s, 2-6-4Ts and the odd 'on loan' or 'borrowed' specimen, like 34102 of Stewarts Lane.

February 1955 saw diesel shunters 13092, 13093 and 13094 working at Hove, Brighton Lower Yard and Lovers Walk, displacing E2 and E3 tanks. Of the latter, 32165, 32166 and 32170 went to store at Horsham. As was now customary the diesels were changed two months later when 13098, 13099, 13100 and 13101 arrived and 13092 departed. In May 13217-13221 (vacuum braked) arrived. After further swaps and changes they settled down to six jobs. 30956, the last remaining Z departed to Exmouth Junction.

In summer 1955 the Oxted Line gained an interval service worked by 2-6-4Ts but the LMS ones, particularly, were not without their problems. M7 30031 arrived from Eastleigh in June 1955. It had greater power than the H class but used more coal in the process, rendering it none-too popular. During that summer, 42104 appeared on the Horsham line, 34047 ventured with a Blackpool special to Willesden whilst the three Atlantics 32421, 32424 and 32426 continued to see regular use. The remaining D3 worked on the Horsham line as late as 11 and 15 September and departed on its last journey to Ashford on 19th, taking E3 32167 with it. The summer Saturday workings for the five Pacifics were three turns to Kensington or Willesden and three along the West Coast. This was rather optimistic considering their availability!

On 19 September, the remainder of the Newhaven duties transferred to Brighton and Newhaven became a 'Stabling Point' for two E4s, an 80XXX tank and the A1X tank on the West Quay. The resulting transfers now gave Brighton sixteen

STEAM LOCOMOTIVES ALLOCATED TO BRIGHTON MAY 1949 until 'closure' 15 June 1964

Class	Type	Numbers	Total
WC/BB	4-6-2	34008/12/3/4/9/27/33/4/5/6/7/8/9/40/1/5/6/7/8	
		34055/7/63/88/9/97/8/9/100/1	Total 29
V	4-4-0	30900/1/2/6/7/11/4/5/6/7/8/9/20/2/3/8/9/30	Total 18
BR 4	4-6-0	75070	Total 1
BR 4	2-6-0	76030/1/2/3/4	Total 5
J1	4-6-2T	32325	Total 1
J2	4-6-2T	32326	Total 1
H1	4-4-2	32039	Total 1
H2	4-4-2	32421/2/4/5/6	Total 5
L	4-4-0	31776/7/8	Total 3
I1X	4-4-2T	32002/5/595	Total 3
I3	4-4-2T	32023/76/80/2/6/8	Total 6
C	0-6-0	31280/724/5	Total 3
C2X	0-6-0	32438/42/3/9/521/3/8/36/8/9/40/3	Total 12
WD	2-8-0	90107/247/345/7/54	Total 5
Q1	0-6-0	33017/37	Total 2
K	2-6-0	32337/8/9/40/1/2/3/4/6/7/8/9	Total 12
M7	0-4-4T	30031/47/8/9/50/1/2/3/4/5/6/109/10/328/79	Total 15
D1	0-4-2T	2253	Total 1
D3	0-4-4T	32365/8/72/6/86/90/3	Total 7
A1X	0-6-0T	32635/6/40/6/55/62/70/8	Total 8
P	0-6-0T	31178/325/556/7/8	Total 5
H	0-4-4T	31005/269/76/9/308/10/9/20/2/530/43/8	Total 12
LM	2-6-2T	41223/30/60/1/76/83/7/91/4/9	
		41300/1/3/5/12/3/4/5/24/5/6/7	Total 22
700	0-6-0	30325/6	Total 2
Q	0-6-0	30531/5/7/43/4/9	Total 6
N	2-6-0	31400/1/2/3/819/20/1/7/8/9/30/1/2/3/59/73	Total 16
U1	2-6-0	31890/1/2/3/4/5/6/8/900/1/2/3/10	Total 13
Z	0-8-0T	30950/5/6	Total 3
E1	0-6-0T	32127/39/42/5/7/606/89	Total 7
E3	0-6-2T	32165/6/7/8/9/70/455	Total 7
E4	0-6-2T	32467/8/70/1/4/5/9/80/1/2/4/5/6/91/4/5/6	
		32502/3/4/5/7/8/9/12/3/4/5/6/8/9/58/62/6	
		32577/8/80/1	Total 38
E5	0-6-2T	32400/567/73/5/83/5/7/8/91/4	Total 10
E5X	0-6-2T	32401/570/6/86	Total 4
E6	0-6-2T	32417/8	Total 2
BR 4	2-6-4T	80010-9/31-4/68/84/5/8/9/94/138-54	Total 37
BR 2	2-6-2T	84024-7	Total 4
LM	2-6-4T	42066/7/75/7/82/5-93/103-6	Total 18
			Grand Total 344

E4s and an allocation of A1Xs which it hadn't had since 32636 left in July 1953. The reduced requirements of the winter service did not stop Atlantic 32421 going to Bournemouth on 30 September. A real stranger on 8 September had been Crosti boilered 92028 which came to Brighton Works for inspection by the staff. It turned on the Preston Park, Hove, Brighton triangle before returning, being banned from the shed yard.

As the winter wore on, the Pacifics got no better and 31894/34090 were 'on loan' to work their stead. An odd sight was Brighton's remaining E5X, 32570, working the 9.30am to Horsham and return, thence 4.36pm to Tunbridge Wells West. With A1Xs now back on the books, one gained the job of coal stage pilot.

As 1956 got underway there was mixed news for the Pacific fleet. On 13 January, 34048 failed at Bournemouth, which sent a T9 4-4-0 back though by early February all five of the Brighton West Countrys were in use. This did not stop H2 32425 going to New Cross Gate with a 'Footex' for Southend Victoria on 17 March. The large engines were needed in April when, for a two week spell, Salisbury turntable was out of use. This meant through engine workings to Exeter and vice versa. This also had the effect of sending Exmouth Junction engines to London Bridge and through East Grinstead (the latter due to engineering work) during their 'layovers' at Brighton. The problems with the Brighton Pacifics can only be ascribed to poor maintenance and it is interesting that the Exeter crews considered the Brighton ones inferior to their own.

The diesel shunters also had their moments and in the early years, spare locos to cover problems were few and far between so Hove Yard had a spell with E4s doing the shunting. May 1956 saw three L class 4-4-0s arrive from Ashford (31776, 31777 and 31778). They were put to use on the Uckfield line and claimed the 7.20am Brighton-London Bridge and 6.38pm Victoria-Brighton.

Disaster befell the Atlantics in May 1956 when in the aftermath of W1 60700's derailment on the Eastern Region, their bogie framing, which was similar, was checked as a precaution. This took 32421 and 32426 out of traffic in August. 32422 and 32425 were not affected and the latter had a busy summer working to both Willesden and Bournemouth. Following the withdrawal of the last D3, the early Sunday morning trips to Seaford and Lewes fell to E4 32484 when the electric current was off.

On 7 July 1956, during a 'Pacific off day', borrowed 80139 took the Plymouth service loaded to twelve bogies. There weren't too many places where a 2-6-4T could cover a 4-6-2 job and get away with it. At least the wheel arrangement was the same bunker first! 73115 and 76059, both ex-works, were also 'borrowed' in August.

The legal battles of the East Grinstead-Lewes line closure are legendary and not for discussion here but having been closed for fourteen months, it reopened on 7 August 1956 and Brighton provided K 32342 and C2X 32442 to work the service, there being insufficient water available for a tank engine. At the end of the summer, E3s 32165 and 32166 returned from Horsham and to regularise the actual position, an Atlantic was now diagrammed to the Bournemouth. The survivor, 32424, now made the job its own, no more having been heard about the Route Restriction.

Unexpectedly, the reimposition of a different restriction for one siding on the quayside at Littlehampton resulted in an A1X being the only loco permitted. With 32655 and 32662 available and one required at Newhaven, 75A could just get by. C class 0-6-0s 31724 and 31725, which had been at the shed from February 1955 until June 1957, came back for the winter 1957/58 on snowplough duties – as they subsequently did for the following two winters. After the 1959 stint, 31724 'hung on' at 75A until November 1961 but 31725 was condemned in August 1960. 31280 joined 31724 for the following season.

On 29 October 1956, the East Grinstead-Lewes reinstated service was revised to reduce tender first running. BR 2-6-4Ts became involved instead - and looked rather odd with just one coach. At the end of the year 80145-80154, all new, came to the shed replacing 42075, which went to Dover and 42106 and 80015-80019, all to Tunbridge Wells West.

The early days of 1957 saw 31725, the snowplough engine, on loan to Tunbridge Wells for a push and pull job – in normal mode we hasten to add – and E2 32101 of Stewarts Lane covering both the Lower Yard and Hove in place of diesel shunters. The three Ls were well used over the Christmas period on van trains and 31776 took out the Plymouth in place of a Pacific six days before Christmas.

The E3s 32165 and 32166 covered the works shunting whilst Departmental 377S was absent and early in the new year both 31776 and 31777 were working to Bournemouth and Salisbury. U1 31898 and Pacific 34066 were 'on loan' to help cover the light Pacifics. Indeed by the first week of June no local 4-6-2s were available and L 31776, Standards 80033 and 80146 plus 73047 and 76029 all had to help out.

1957 was a fairly stable year so far as allocations were concerned, the shed suffering only a net loss of two M7s and two C2Xs (all to Three Bridges) and one class P tank to Eastleigh. It was 204HP shunter 11222 which came to 75A for Kingston Wharf Duty (778) arriving on 12 May which pushed the small tank out, after the necessary crew training, at the end of June. The diesel was accommodated overnight in the transit shed at Shoreham.

Matters were reversed somewhat

on 10 August when the Works Terrier 377S had to cover the Littlehampton shunt as no 'normal' A1X was available. Through all this, the remaining Atlantic, 32424, was quite happily covering the London van jobs, Saturday trains to Willesden and, of course, the Bournemouth, although there is still no record of the route restriction being removed. A roof was provided over the shed coal stage in September 1957 causing coaling to be done temporarily at the north end of the shed. At the end of October, two of the L 4-4-0s, 31777 and 31778, were put to store at Newhaven. They came out again for the Christmas vans. As 1957 draws to a close, it is time for an update on the allocation at the end of the year:

WC 4-6-2: 34039, 34045, 34046, 34047, 34048
H2 4-4-2: 32424
L 4-4-0: 31776, 31777, 31778
C 0-6-0: 31724, 31725
C2X 0-6-0: 32442, 32449, 32521, 32540
K 2-6-0: 32338-32343
M7 0-4-4T: 30031, 30054, 30055
LM 2-6-4T: 42082, 42103
BR 2-6-4T: 80010, 80011, 80031, 80032, 80033, 80145-80154
E4 0-6-2T: 32467, 32468, 32475, 32481, 32484, 32485, 32494, 32502, 32503, 32504, 32509, 32512, 32515, 32562, 32566, 32577
A1X 0-6-0T: 32655, 32662
P 0-6-0T: 31556
Total 60

As we enter 1958, Pacifics were again rostered for the Bournemouth job and from March, the 1.55pm to London and 6.10 Victoria return (an infamously poor timekeeper and the subject of much comment from its clientele) were also booked for the 'big engines'. Push and pull working ceased on the Steyning line from 6 March 1958. The use of E4s increased. Push/pull stock was still used, with the loco 'running round' at each end of the journey. For the summer service, an hourly interval service was introduced on the Horsham-Steyning-Brighton line. This required three M7s from Brighton and two from Horsham.

So how did 1958 work out? The remaining Atlantic went in May having been active on London vans early in the year and then kept for a farewell 'Rail Tour'. The Ls worked to both Bournemouth and London. The K class, ever reliable, were on passenger work to Eastbourne, Redhill and London Bridge in July. Whilst the intentions were good with the 6.10pm from Victoria, the reality was somewhat different with BR 2-6-4Ts covering Pacifics. K class 32343 went up with the 1.55pm on 11 October – being a Saturday the 6.10pm return would not be involved! Borrowed U 2-6-0s plus the Ls looked after the Bournemouth. With the Hastings line dieselisation and reductions in requirements at St Leonards, Brighton gained Schools 30900 and 30901 in May and these two were of use for the West Coast services and Saturday inter-regional trains. The class was cleared for use on the Uckfield line in mid-1958. Additional to these, 30909 and 30936 were on loan in the autumn. Pacifics 34045 and 34047 were both in works for 'Generals and rebuilding' and did not come back, being exchanged with 34008 and 34019 from Nine Elms.

The Littlehampton shunting job still produced a few surprises with the P 0-6-0T having a go on 4 November. A new job for the Ls in the autumn was the Lingfield Race Specials.

1959 was a year of more change. New shunter D2082 came to Kingston Wharf in March replacing little P tank 31325 which had covered the loss of 11222 to Eastleigh in August 1958 (for Winchester). Pacifics 34039, 34046 and 34048 all went away for rebuilding, replaced by 34097, 34098 and 34099 from Bournemouth. Four more schools (30914, 30915, 30916 and 30917) from Ramsgate and Nine Elms came in to replace the Ls which went to London. Unexpectedly, two more LM 2-6-4Ts came in February, 42066 and 42067 from Three Bridges together with BR Standard 4-6-0 75070, the latter being too long for the platform at London Bridge on its allocated job at 75E. Standard tanks 80010, 80011 and 80012 went to Three Bridges in exchange. 75070 did do some useful work with the 7.19am to London Bridge and 4.40pm return, but being a 'one off' at the

Rugged, competent and popular; one of the Ks, under the great tank and that wonderful clock, 11 September 1960. 32340 came from Fratton in December 1950 and spent twelve years here until despatched by the accountants. Photograph Peter Groom.

shed it only just lasted the year out and went back whence it came the following January.

Early in the year, on 12 January, the Departmental A1X came to the main shed with the closure of Brighton Works (Duty 769). The M7 fleet changed but overall, six remained on the books, 75A finishing the year with 30047, 30049, 30050, 30051, 30056 and 30110. Meanwhile, in the aftermath of the Kent Coast electrification reshuffle, seven H 0-4-4s had crept back in, being more popular with the Brighton men. Four remained at the year end, 31276, 31308, 31530 and 31543. The E4 fleet was reduced by five during the year and the last two E3s at the shed went to Norwood. Old Brighton favourites U1s 31890 and 31891 which had gone to 'The Brick' in June 1951 came back exactly eight years later and at the end of the year, the remaining LM 2-6-4Ts went to their 'proper' Region in exchange for standard ones. In Brighton's case 42066, 42067, 42082 and 42103 departed.

On the traffic side, the Bournemouth service was cancelled as an 'economy measure' from 5 January until 2 May 1959. Diesel shunter D3669 was tested at Lewes on 4 August and, together with D3094 at Newhaven took over two E4 jobs. The number of E4s was reduced by five during 1959 but that did not stop 32562 working a passenger from Eastbourne to Hastings on 8 August. The class was not unknown either as Eastbourne Goods Pilot. On 6 July Horsham lost its allocation and M7s 30047-30051 came to Brighton with their duties. Horsham remained as a stabling point. By September there were six Schools and five Pacifics for four summer and three winter jobs.

The changeover of Pacifics continued into 1960 with 34038, 34055 and 34057 coming in to replace 34097, 34098 and 34099. 34008 did better in that it was rebuilt and came back to Brighton in July. During that year, the Schools swapped about but overall remained at six. 30914, 30915 and 30916 went to Redhill in April; 30902, 30918 and 30919 came from Nine Elms but further changes in November sent 30902 and 30918 back to be replaced at Brighton by 30907 and 30911. In the midst of all this changing about, BR Standards 76053, 76054 and 76055 were covering some of the Brighton jobs. Two more Ks 'came home' in September when 32337 and 32344, both of which had been away some six years returned to Brighton and the 'auto train' fleet was boosted by three more M7s and another H.

More shunters came in February in the shape of D2281, D2282 and D2286; they covered Eastbourne (including Crumbles Ballast Hole) in place of an E4, Brighton Top and Lower Yard Trip and Shunt and Kingston Wharf, the Eastbourne one being changed fortnightly from the Brighton pool. The P tank served as Brighton Works Shunter for a while.

The brave little E4s were still working the Wolverhampton-Eastbourne service east of Brighton on Saturdays until the service finished at the end of October. 32479 had a brief moment of glory working the 4.02pm passenger from Brighton to Eastbourne on Christmas Eve.

The following year, 1961, the last Cs went to Ashford in November and the last C2X (32449) to Three Bridges in February. The M7s all went too, seven in April and two in June. The Hs had already departed, in January; 31005, 31276, 31308, 31322 and 31530 going to Tonbridge and Ivatt 2-6-2Ts 41300, 41301, 41303 and 41305 arrived. 41291 followed in April and 41260, 41261, 41283 and 41287 in June. 41305 only stayed until March but even more, 41324, 41325, 41326 and 41327, came in September.

For the 1961/62 winter, 700 class 30325 and 30326 were the snowplough engines. Further 0-6-0s to arrive were Q class 30535 and 30544 in the summer and 30537 and 30549 in December. The two U1s (31890 and 31891) departed in September. As part of a general switch round of 2-6-0s, four Ns (31819, 31820, 31821 and 31859) arrived in June, only to depart in

'Spot The Join' composite in May 1947, skilfully assembled in the cutting edge laboratories of Irwell Press. From left to right we have the coaling stage and the re-roofed 1938 asbestos sheeted northlight pattern shed roof which originally had arched entrances to each road. Looks were not improved by opening up the east side roads to the elements. In the foreground is the wheeldrop/engine hoist for wheel removals. The building to the right behind the water tank was originally a four road carriage shed but by the turn of the century had become a wagon shop. When the Carriage and Wagon Department moved out to Lancing (1912/13) it became Brighton Works 'Stock Shed'. Later, it was turned over to the 'running' authorities but following the 1930s electrification it became a workshop for the Road Motor Engineer, in whose hands it remained until June 1964. Top right is London Road viaduct on the 'East' route towards Lewes. To the right of the water tank and the steaming loco is the post-electrification signal box together with its access bridge. To the left of the box, the eagle-eyed will see one of the Southern's vitreous enamel BRIGHTON boards attached to the Works wall. Interesting locos in view include a WD 2-8-0 and a Schools 4-4-0. Photographs Derek Clayton.

November and be replaced by 31400-31403. Two new classes, in the form of E6s 32417 and 32418 and BR standard 2-6-2Ts 84024-84027 arrived in May. These moves were sufficient to reduce the E4s to six by the end of the year, 32468, 32479, 32503, 32509, 32558 and 32580. The E6s worked to Kemp Town, assisted at Lancing and did a bit of local freight work. The Standard tanks made a few appearances on the Horsham branch.

On the big engine side in 1961, rebuilt 34027 arrived with transfer of work from Bricklayers Arms in May and 'original' 34038 departed for Exmouth Junction in November. Brighton still retained five; at the end of the year these were 34008, 34019, 34027, 34055 and 34057. The Schools underwent their usual travels with 30919 condemned in January, replaced by 30920. September saw the demise of 30907 and November 30920. However, 30922, 30923 and 30928 arrived in October and 30929, 30930 in December, of which 30922 only lasted a month. 30911 departed for Redhill in December leaving seven of the 4-4-0s on the books at 75A at the year end.

From 4 December 1961 the 7.17am to London Bridge and 4.40 back was diagrammed to a Pacific (instead of a Schools). Just a fortnight before the situation was such that an LM 2-6-2T worked the 8.20am Brighton-Victoria! In 1962, the Brighton-Bournemouth job went back to a Schools after its mid-winter suspension but there were still surprises in store. 32636 (A1X) went to Eastbourne in mid-June to cover the Yard Pilot and Crumbles branch in place of D2283 which had failed. E4 32503 covered Newhaven Middle Yard Pilot on 29 July instead of an Ivatt 2-6-2T: there was still the odd E4 on the Brighton-Horsham-Guildford workings (such as 32479 on 24 September) and steam still appeared on the Lewes shunting turn. Hove Yard closed on 5 November 1962, releasing a shunting loco.

1962, it will be recalled, was 'The year of the Accountant' when whole classes disappeared at the stroke of his pen. At Brighton, the Schools and Ks were the victims at the year end but before that, the 700s went in January after so-called 'snow clearance' duties – the plough provided for 30325 did not fit. Three of the Qs went in June and the last (30531) in November. With the demise of the Ks, the Ns were increased to twelve, mostly from the West of England and more U1s arrived (some only for a brief stay). The E6s also went in December and the E4s were down to four, more LM tanks, 41223, 41230 and 41276 arriving to replace them. Even at this late stage, further locos would turn up – such as BR Standard 4s 76030-76034, which had been pushed around by the Eastern Region since dieselisation of the GE Section. They replaced the U1s.

During 1962 the Pacific fleet increased to no less than ten with the transfer of 34012, 34013, 34014 and 34101 from Bricklayers Arms, 34089 and 34100 from Stewarts Lane, with the loss of only 34008 to Eastleigh. The engines from London were the result of transferring the Central Division work away from London sheds. Yet it seemed that however many Pacifics Brighton had, it could never provide a full complement for the day. On 4 and 5 December 1962 for example, only two out of the ten were available leaving 30916, just days from condemnation, to work the 11.30 Plymouth as far as Salisbury.

At the end of 1962 Brighton boasted 71 locos on the books which, apart from the ten Pacifics, were made up of: fifteen Ivatt 2-6-2Ts, seventeen BR Standard 2-6-4Ts, twelve N 2-6-0s, five BR 4 2-6-0s, four U1s, four E4s and four Terriers.

1963 was the year when the Type 3 D6500 diesels really began make their presence felt; indeed, by mid-July no less than nineteen of them were working on the Central Division. The E4s finally departed from 75A in June 1963 when 32479 was withdrawn. Prior to that 32468 and 32503 were working the 'Lancing Belle' and 32474 and 32479 were working at Hove. 32479 also covered the shunting job at Lewes in place of a diesel.

For the Terriers 1963 was also the last year at 75A. 32635 was withdrawn in March and three, 32636, 32662 and 32670, departed to Eastleigh (for the Hayling Island branch) in May, replaced by 32640 and 32678 which stayed until August and October respectively. 32640 was working on the wharf at Littlehampton in mid-June and 32678 at Newhaven in July. The West Side Tramway at Newhaven closed with 32678 clearing the final vehicles on 10 August. 32678 left for its parent shed on 18 August and had a spell as shed pilot before withdrawal on 5 October.

So far as the Pacifics were concerned, 34063 came from Exmouth Junction in May to replace 34055 which was withdrawn and 34101 was 'swapped' with Nine Elms for 34088 in June, though it stayed only a month. The remaining 'big engines' (34012, 34013, 34014, 34019, 34027, 34057, 34063, 34089, 34100) all went to Salisbury in September when the Brighton-Plymouth train was covered to and from Salisbury by an Exmouth Junction loco which also took the night 'filling in' turn to Norwood and back. 'The Bournemouth' went over to a D6500 on Saturdays as did the 3.20am News from London Bridge and the Cardiff service ceased running for the winter. The last diagrammed Pacific on the Oxted line was the summer 7.17am Brighton-London Bridge (which 34013 worked on 29 June). 34012 worked to Willesden during the summer, 34013 managed the Eastbourne-Glasgow sleeper away from Eastbourne on 10 August and 34057 worked a relief Newhaven-Victoria Boat train on 2 August. There was no booked steam to Victoria after the end of July.

The Ivatt 2-6-2Ts changed over in March 1963 when 41223, 41230, 41276, 41283 and 41291 went west to Barnstaple and Exmouth Junction, replaced by 41294, 41299, 41312, 41313 and 41314. The last two, it will be remembered, had left Brighton for Exmouth Junction eleven years before. 41261 and 41324 went to Weymouth during the summer leaving fourteen Ivatts to soldier on into 1964. In the course of 1963 the N 2-6-0s were reduced from twelve to just three, although they still appeared on the 8.20am Brighton-Victoria now and again. The U1s were cleared out completely but not before 31890, 31901 and 31910 had a spell on the 1.38pm Hove-Victoria van train, and the 3.27 and 5.13am News trains from London. From 17 June the van train passed to the Ns. Another job the Ns performed was the clearance of condemned coaching stock from Ardingly on the Horsted Keynes branch. 31831 and 31873 were so employed on 11 October. The BR Standard 4s all went to Guildford in September. They did do some useful work from Brighton such as covering the 7.55am Brighton-Redhill via Tonbridge and the Eastbourne-Sheffield Saturdays service as far as Kensington.

Dieselisation came to the Oxted line in two stages, from 6 May and 17 June 1963. The main impact was on the BR 80000 tanks – Tunbridge Wells West shed closed on 9 September 1963 as a consequence and twelve of the 2-6-Ts came to Brighton. A further six came from Stewarts Lane making no less the 29 of them on the 75A books, of which 21 departed by the end of the year. Once the 2-6-4Ts had been sorted out and others despatched to Redhill, Eastleigh, Weymouth and Feltham, by the year end just eight were left at Brighton (80010, 80011, 80013, 80014, 80016-80019). The last four had been based at Brighton back in 1952. Like all schemes of dieselisation there were teething troubles and 80031 replaced a DMU on 16 October – doubtless there were other such instances. Newhaven shed, latterly only a stabling point, closed the same day as Tunbridge Wells. The snowplough engines for 1963 were Q 0-6-0s 30531 and 30543. In fact one was stored at Brighton and one at Redhill for the worst of the winter! They both subsequently did some work at Redhill before being officially transferred from Brighton in May 1964. So, into 1964, the final year of steam allocation at Brighton. The year started with a complement of twenty-seven:

Q 0-6-0: 30531, 30543
N 2-6-0: 31829, 31830, 31832
Ivatt 2-6-2T: 41230, 41260, 41287, 41294, 41299, 41300, 41301, 41302, 41312, 41313, 41314, 41325, 41326, 41327
BR 2-6-4T: 80010, 80011, 80013, 80014, 80016, 80017, 80018, 80019.

More Type 3s came to the Division early in 1964 (making a total of thirty-six) and the three N 2-6-0s did not last out the first month. Regular steam power ceased on the Brighton main line on 4 January 1964. Three Bridges shed closed 5 January 1964 leaving it as a stabling point for a handful of 2-6-4Ts from Brighton which were changed over on the 8.30pm Brighton-Horsham. Horsham continued as a 'sub' of Brighton with four Ivatt 2-6-2Ts working passenger trains on the Steyning and Guildford lines.

The Brighton-Plymouth was now running via Portsmouth and 2-6-4Ts 80014, 80017 and 80019 all took a turn on this one, otherwise their work was relatively 'menial' such as the breakdown vans, plus the Three Bridges changeovers. The Ivatt 2-6-2Ts worked the Horsham jobs and the 'Lancing Belle' which was now a six coach single engine load (previously eleven in the days of pairs of E4s). The Horsham-Brighton line was dieselised on 4

That massive tank and two Moguls on shed, K class 32349 of Fratton and U1 31905 of Stewarts Lane. The period would be about 1957, as 31905 has just had the revised crest applied to the tender.

May when 41287, 41294, 41299 and 41301 were transferred to Guildford for the remaining jobs on the Guildford-Horsham branch (for which two locos were outstationed at Horsham).

The summer service on 15 June 1964 saw '75A' lose its allocation. The Ivatt 2-6-2Ts went to Salisbury, Bournemouth and Eastleigh and the Standard tanks to Redhill, Eastleigh, Bournemouth and Feltham. Redhill now supplied the remaining loco required at Three Bridges. The 'Lancing Belle' was hauled by a D6500 from 15 June and ceased completely on 3 July. Staff then had to use the normal EMU to Lancing station and walk the rest. Water and the turntable remained available in Brighton shed yard for a while but it was necessary for locos to travel to Redhill for any attention, or for coal. This lasted until spring 1966.

The last steam locomotive to visit Brighton in normal service was, strangely enough, a former Brighton engine, 34012, with a Blandford Forum special on 11 June 1966. The shed was demolished during August 1966 but the odd steam locomotive did arrive in the station on Rail Tours and so on until March 1967. Shunting locos were retained on the allocation until May 1973 when they were finally transferred to Selhurst (3220, 3222 and 3226).

The Men

Main line work at Brighton took the men to Bournemouth West and Salisbury, plus London turns to Victoria and London bridge via Eridge and Uckfield. They worked 'Main Line' to Clapham Junction via Gatwick and East Croydon, then on to Kensington and Willesden Mitre Bridge Junction with the cross country services to the West Midlands and North West. Van trains to New Cross Gate and freights to Norwood Yard were covered and one trip took them via Haywards Heath to Horsted Keynes with a K 2-6-0.

On the West Coast, Brighton men worked to Portslade, Hove, Shoreham, Worthing and Chichester, a 'frontier' post between the Central and LSW Divisions for freight, and also to Beeding Cement Works and to Littlehampton. East Coast work took them to Lewes, Polegate and Eastbourne but not normally beyond.

The local passenger work consisted of the 'motor' to Horsham and included work across the branch to Guildford. There was also a turn from Horsham to Three Bridges, keeping up useful route knowledge. Heading further to the north-east, there was work to Tonbridge via Tunbridge Wells. Shunting kept them occupied at the local shed and works, also at Kemp Town, Kingston Wharf (Shoreham) and at the Pullman Car works.

Finally, there was the 'Lancing Belle', the workmen's train of antique coaches, provided since 1919 after protests when the Carriage and Wagon Department moved from Brighton to Lancing. This was normally double headed by two E4s.

The Coastal and Cross Country Services

The 'Coast Line Express' dated from 1912 when it ran from Brighton to Bournemouth and Salisbury, with a Plymouth coach in the Salisbury portion. It was withdrawn in the First World War. In 1922, it was revived as a joint LBSC/LSW/GW venture running at 11.00am from Brighton to Cardiff, Ilfracombe and Bournemouth. It split at Portsmouth with one portion going to Salisbury where it divided again for Cardiff and Ilfracombe. The other part ran from Portsmouth to Southampton and Bournemouth. Coaches from all three participating companies were used.

After World War II there were three separate trains leaving Brighton for Bournemouth, Cardiff and Plymouth. They were withdrawn or reduced to weekends only a few times, due to fuel shortages or as an economy measure and only the Plymouth survived 'Beeching'. This too was cut back to Exeter. Whilst Brighton Pacifics were allocated to these jobs for most of the time from 1948 onwards, their availability meant the reality was somewhat different as our look through the years shows.

Type 3 D6500 diesels took over partly from 1963 and the Bullied/Raworth Co-Cos played a part between Brighton and Fratton the following year. There was a brief return to steam in 1966 after Brighton shed had closed to such traction. The Brighton-Exeter service became 'SO' and for a while was made up of a six car Hastings DEMU. Eventually, the ubiquitous D6500s (class 33s) took over with eight coaches. In the opposite direction, 1912 also saw the start of a Brighton-Hastings-Ashford-Folkestone-Dover-Walmer-Deal service. The Dover portion was not restored after the Great War but Brighton-Ashford continued until the East Coast electrification of 1935. In the summer of 1912 a 'South Coast Express' ran from Hastings to Portsmouth Harbour – in spite of the restriction on through working from east to west via Brighton station. It conveyed four LSW coaches, was worked by a tank engine and at times was, of necessity, shunted between platforms at Brighton.

Looking at the cross country 'north to south' side of things, the 'Sunny South Special' went back to 1905 with portions from Manchester and Liverpool joining at Crewe, a Birmingham part at Rugby, thence via Willesden Junction and through to Eastbourne via Brighton. LBSC locos worked from Willesden Junction. After World War II there were several through services from the north and Midlands to Sussex via the same route until the early 1960s. Brighton shed played a large part in their working south of Willesden, or in some cases, Kensington.

To complete the cross country picture, there was a Birkenhead-Hastings service via Reading, Redhill and Brighton from the Grouping to 1939 and it was subsequently restored after the War's end. Through coaches did not go beyond Eastbourne after spring 1962 and the service was withdrawn completely in autumn that year. It was restored briefly in 1964, running to and from Wolverhampton only. It finally ceased in September that year.

Acknowledgements to 'The Railway Observer' and 'Southern Region Engine Workings' (Ian Allan) by Chris Gammell. Thanks also to Eric Youldon.

More of Those Big Engines at Crewe

Notes by Allan C. Baker

Above, below and top right. An attractive sequence showing Princess Royal Pacific 46203 PRINCESS MARGARET ROSE in March 1960 at Crewe. The train is one from Liverpool to Euston, but unfortunately we do not know which one; however, as the engine carries no headboard we can assume it is not a named train – though there were occasions when the headboards were not carried for one reason or another. It is in all probability the 11am ex-Liverpool Lime Street, due away from Crewe at 12 noon and into Euston at 3.17pm. 46203 was, so to speak, the first *(continued below)*

of the 'production' batch of these engines, as opposed to the two original members, built after a gap of almost two years, and with several modifications. For example the arrangement of reversing reach rods was different, with a longer primary rod and a support at its mid-length – there was also a different method of supporting the expansion link. The first view shows the train shortly after arrival at Platform 4 and the other two on leaving, the crew leaning out of the cab for the benefit of the photographer! This engine alternated between Edge Hill and Crewe North for much of the 1950s and of course Edge Hill had Princess Royals on its allocation for many years specifically for its London diagrams. The engine is not taking on water (doubtless the crew were intending to get a *(continued top right)* tender full on Whitmore troughs) and somebody has left the tender tank filler door open. These pictures bring back particular memories for me, as the very first time I went to London was when Dad took me there for the day, among other things to visit the annual Model Engineer Exhibition. We travelled by local train to Stafford and caught the early morning Crewe to Euston train there, hauled by 46203 – this would have been about 1957-58, when it was allocated to Crewe North. I can see her now running into No.1 platform at Stafford, then in its old form and prior to the extensive rebuilding as part of the modernisation and electrification of the West Coast Main Line. Photographs D.H. Beecroft, The Transport Treasury.

Another of the 'production' engines, this time 46206 PRINCESS MARIE LOUISE, again leaving Crewe for the south, about 1960. Judging by the lack of coal at the front of the tender, the engine has worked the train in from the north, so it may be a Liverpool train, despite in all probability the engine being a Crewe North allocated one at the time. This was the only member of the class fitted with a coal pusher tender, like the later Duchess engines; observe the twin exhaust pipes and cover over the operating valves on the rear of the tender coal space, which also has its water filler door left open! The train is standing at the south end of No.5 platform; AWS battery box has appeared just in front of the cab and the associated timing reservoir in front of it. Photograph Jim Hardy, courtesy John Bucknall.

46250

Top left. Splendid view at the south end of Crewe Station. Duchess Pacific 46250 CITY OF LICHFIELD was a Carlisle Upperby engine at the time and had been allocated there since June 1958. It is running back light to the North Shed along No.3 down through road. No coal is visible in the tender and doubtless the engine will have brought a train in from the north, perhaps the one seen just behind in No.3 platform with the Type 4 diesel at its head. Picture taken I would say in late 1961 or 1962; the English Electric Type 4 diesel has the split indicator boxes first introduced on D324, new in July 1961, but it does not yet sport the yellow warning panel introduced in 1962. Photograph The Transport Treasury.

Above. The Ivatt-modified Duchess Pacific 46256 SIR WILLIAM A STANIER FRS, on Crewe North shed in April 1964. The engine stands on one of the preparation pits at the west end of the shed yard. Notice the Great Western tender engine in front; unusual this, for at this period Western Region steam engines usually only turned up at Crewe on freight or parcels jobs, and thus generally found their way to the South Shed rather than the North. Items to note on the Duchess are the roller bearing axle boxes on the tender and trailing truck with the mileage recorder on the leading tender axle box. The square component between the tender axles is the feed box and filter for the exhaust injector, itself seen just under the cab and behind the trailing truck with its cast 'Delta' frame. Originally these trucks on this and 46257 were fabricated, but they suffered from fracturing and were thus replaced by castings. Notice too, the non-adjustable spring hangers on the tender. Only this engine and sister 46257 had these – they made spring changing a much easier operation, with no large nuts to run up and down partially seized screw threads! Photograph D.H. Beecroft, The Transport Treasury.

Left. SIR WILLIAM A STANIER FRS at Crewe North on Sunday 27 September 1964. The previous day it had worked the RCTS special train, The Scottish Lowlander, to and from Carlisle, and this was the last duty of any of the class in BR service. The locomotive had just enough steam left on the Sunday morning to move itself out of the Middle Shed so that John Bucknall and a few others could get shots like this. All other members of the class had been withdrawn a couple of weeks earlier, but 46256 had been kept in service for this one last occasion. Notice how the AWS electrical conduit has been 'dog-legged' around the reversing gear, this locomotive and sister 46257 having a different reversing arrangement from the remainder of the class, utilising circular shafts and universal couplings. One of the latter can just be discerned to the rear of the semi-circular cover which housed the reversing screw itself – it was not in the cab as was normal practice. Notice too the twin brake block arrangement. The very early members of the class did not have this. With this type of gear the top block always wore more than the bottom one, so when changing the blocks we used to put the bottom block in the top position and fit a new one at the bottom – good Crewe North economy. The later Class 5s had the same arrangement, as did many of the Standard engines. Looking at this superb close up of the cylinders and motion work, it's difficult to imagine that this locomotive was never to turn a wheel under its own steam again – when it came to putting it back in the shed later that day, there was insufficient steam left and it had to be pushed by another engine. I paid my last respects the following afternoon when she was still warm and I spent a melancholy fifteen minutes or so on the footplate in the driver's seat! By this time other survivors, assembled at Crewe North after their last rites, were all stabled in the remains of 'Abba' shed, already bereft of name and number plates, with motion removed and stacked in the tenders awaiting the call of the scrap man; it was not long in coming. This engine was similarly shorn of it vitals later that week, and moved to join its sisters. Oh, what would she be worth today! Photograph John Bucknall.

CHARING CROSS UNDER ROCKET ATTACK

The Hungerford Bridge and Charing Cross suffered like no other London terminus in the Second World War. On one terrible night in April 1941 a high explosive bomb had struck the hotel and more than a hundred incendiaries had put much of the station, including three trains and a fourth on Hungerford Bridge, to the fire. As is famously recorded in 'War On The Line' by Bernard Darwin the situation was only saved by the staff and a redoubtable Coventry Climax Trailer Pump. Matters were coming to a hideous head with the flames approaching an unexploded land mine stuck by its parachute on the bridge. The water supply failed and with the flames only twelve feet from

WAR REPORT...WAR REPORT...WAR REPORT...WAR

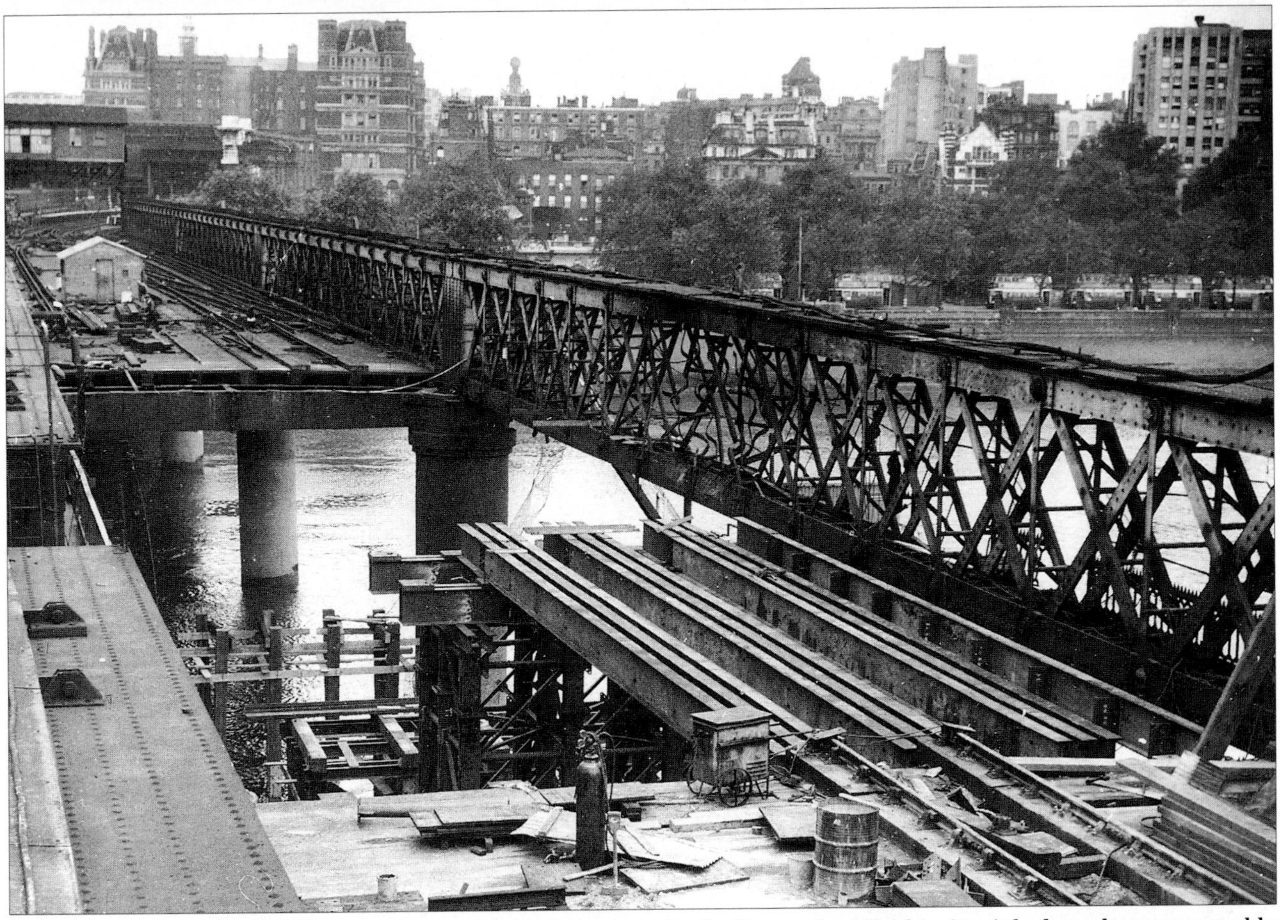

the land mine the Fire Brigade arrived to finally beat them back. Hungerford Bridge, it might have been reasonably hoped, would have an easier time after that but it was not to be. Three years later, on 18 June 1944, a V1 rocket in a direct hit punched this gaping hole (left and top right). The explosion shredded ironwork, smashed the steel deck and threw rails around like sticks while the signal gantry survived relatively unscathed. Reconstruction was well underway a few months later (bottom right) on 5 September 1944.

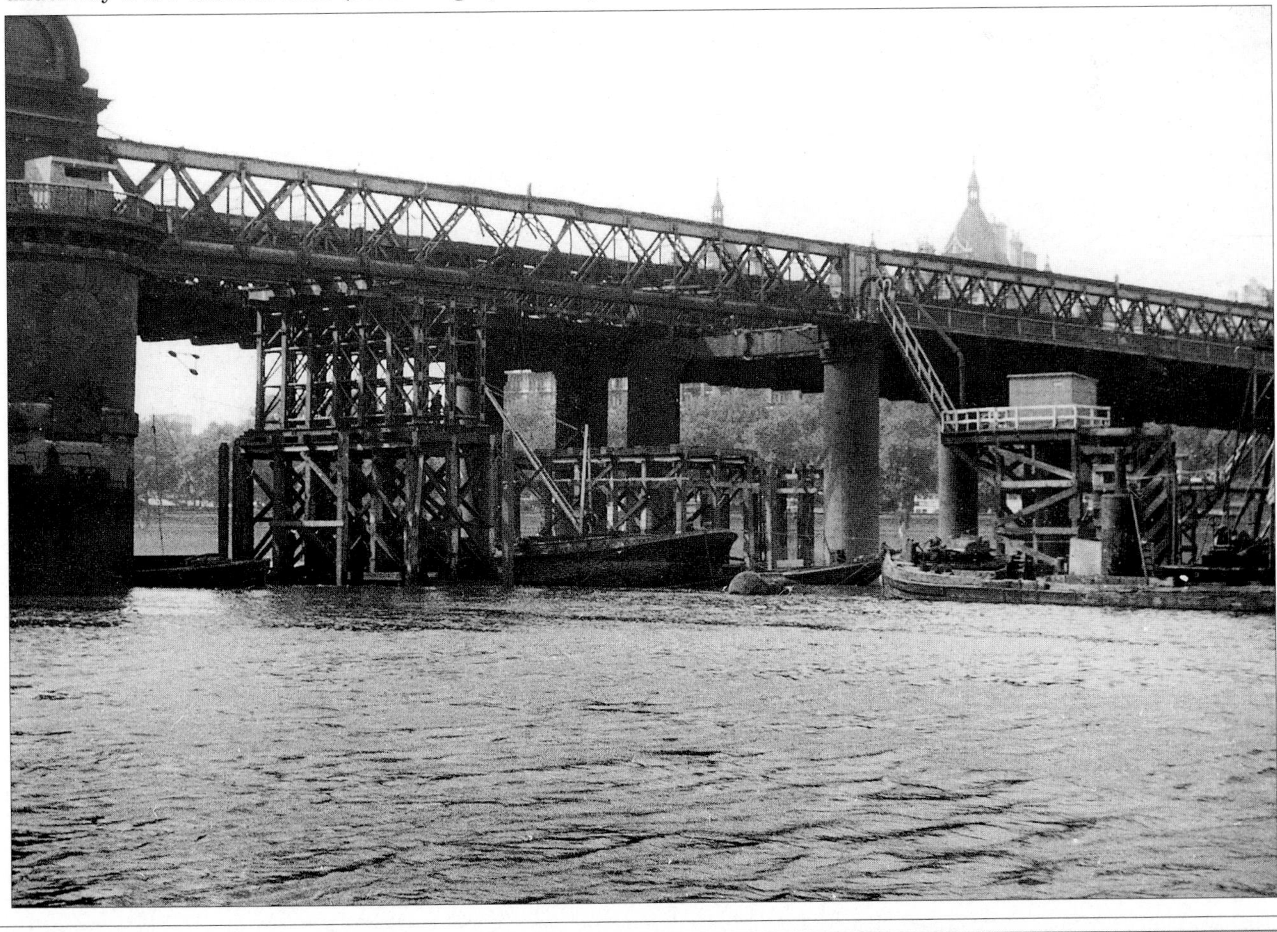

A4s At Home

Left. There were always, of course, plenty of Pacifics to be found at Top Shed, Kings Cross; in fact, so constrained and closely-bounded was the place that it was literally crowded with Pacifics. All the English A4s could be seen in a season or so and a few of the Haymarket ones too, with luck. On 9 September 1959 60034 LORD FARINGDON (AWS fitted by now but with 'curly' non-Gill sans 6 on the front – it got the correct 6 during its later time in Scotland) stands next to fellow Kings Cross resident 60006 SIR RALPH WEDGWOOD, both ready for the next job north. Photograph R.F. Smith, The Transport Treasury.

Below left. The shed itself was a curious affair, marked by the remnants of a vast elliptical shed, 'the Crescent' of more than twenty roads, originating in the 1850s. The bare bones of this survived in much amended form to the end of steam, accompanied by a more conventional straight shed which dated in turn from the 1860s. Various improvements came over the years, such as a new roof and modern arrangements in the yard but despite all this it can be seen that Kings Cross remained an unconventionally laid out depot. 60022 MALLARD stands by the nearest (south) wall of the straight shed and there are two more A4s at the rear. The high sidings with the smoke from a shunting engine in the far background are part of the North London line.

Below. 60023 GOLDEN EAGLE being readied outside the shed on 9 September 1959. The roof as first built in the early 1860s had had transverse pitches; this conventional rearrangement was made by BR in 1949. The gantry on the right supplied water across several servicing roads after the fashion of New England (featured many times in *British Railways Illustrated*) and was built at the time of the upgrading of the shed yard. Photograph R.F. Smith, The Transport Treasury.

Top right. 60028 WALTER K. WHIGHAM on 9 September 1959, three days before the end of Elizabethan running that year; the engine had been a principal performer that year. WALTER, at Haymarket for periods before the War, had been at Kings Cross since May 1948 and was one of those to go before Top Shed finally closed to steam in June 1963; he was withdrawn some months before, at the end of 1962. Photograph R.F. Smith, The Transport Treasury.

Below. 60030 GOLDEN FLEECE on 19 September 1959; from its condition it has obviously worked a very important train in the last few days, though it did not play a part in the Elizabethan that season. Photograph R.F. Smith, The Transport Treasury.

Below right. Wings severely clipped, 60021 WILD SWAN on 9 September 1959 has a while to wait until its next flight north. Photograph R.F. Smith, The Transport Treasury.

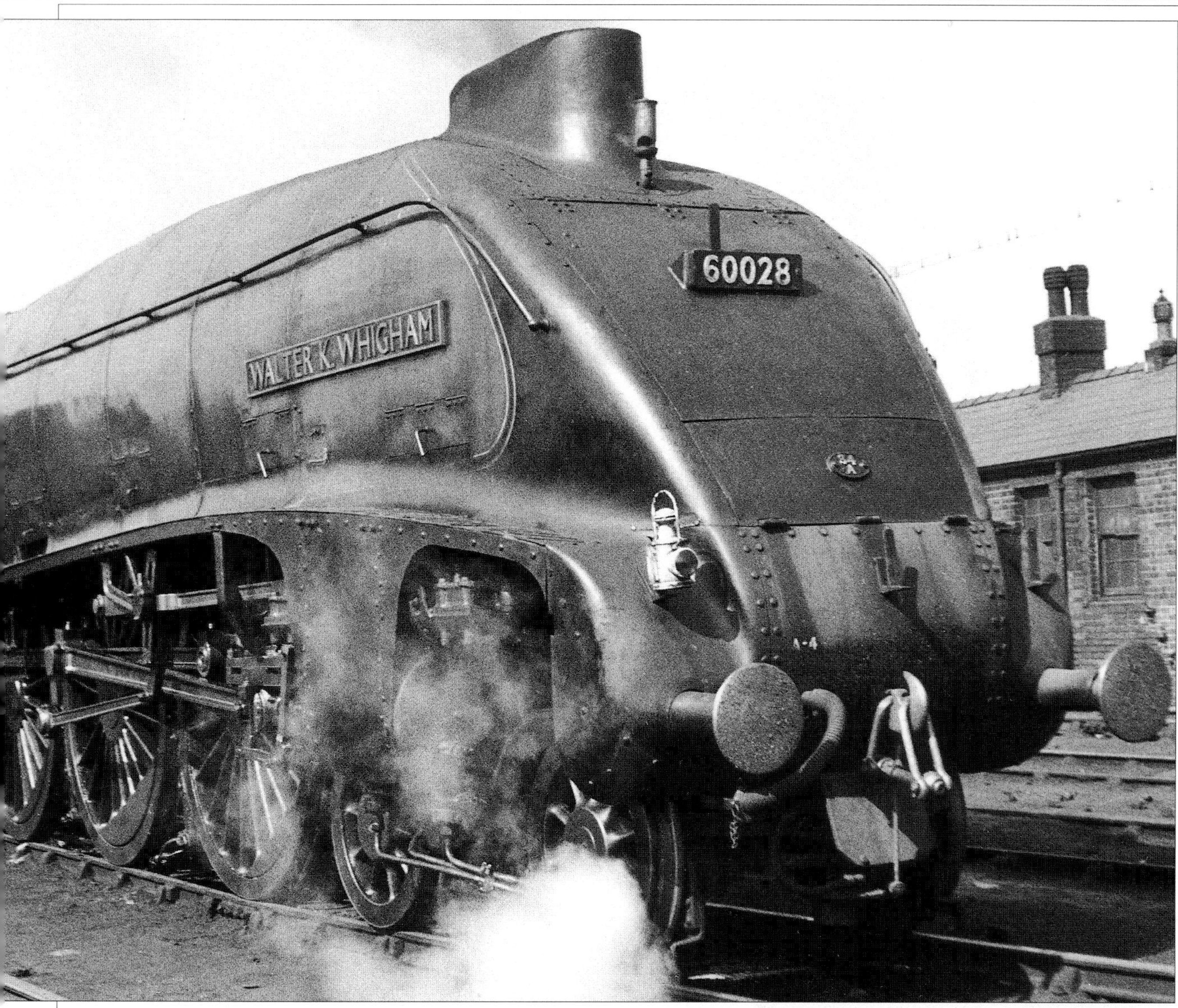
60028
WALTER K. WHIGHAM
A-4

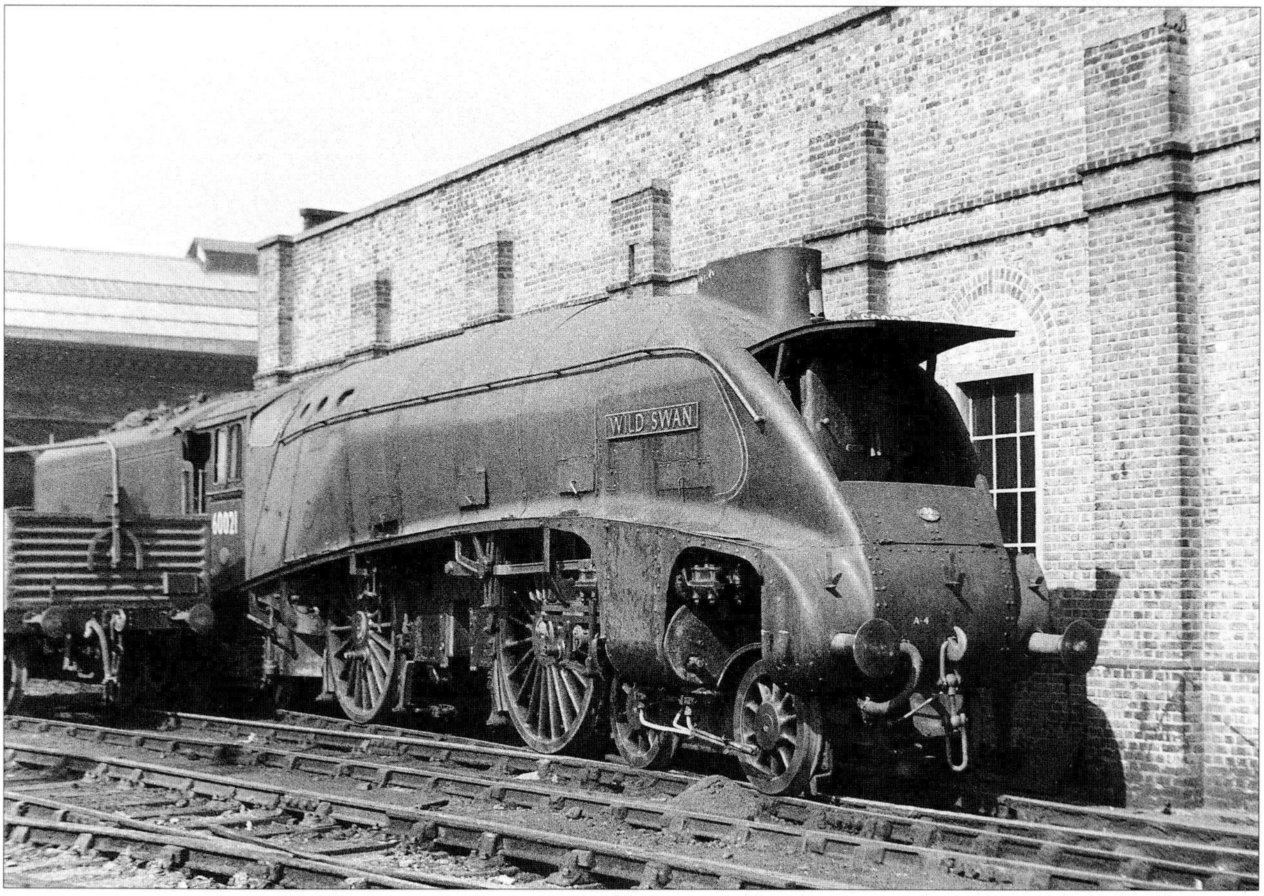
WILD SWAN
60021
A-4

FOURUM It's a People Thing

It's easy to forget the people when it comes to the glorious detail and sheer ironmongery of the railway – so here are a few, from 'all sides' as it were. The clothes, the bicycles, the spectacles, all are firmly of another age. The workers with their bicycles are 'plodding, snail-like, their weary way' at Southampton in 1966 (though you could be forgiven for thinking it was a lot earlier) while the crowds with their bags are tramping out into the dubious delights of Old

Euston's surrounding streets in 1955. The chap oiling the signal is at Oxford in 1965 and 'the pack' with their cameras and macs are photographing 35011 GENERAL STEAM NAVIGATION at Shillingstone on an LCGB tour in the 1960s. Photographs (except Euston) J.A.M. Vaughn, The Transport Treasury.

GARRATT GLIMPSES

Just what would the collective noun for Garratts be? They're not often photographed together – they were just too big for that – but here are three at outside an ex-Midland roundhouse – Cricklewood most likely – headed by 4970. This was one of the 'production batch' of thirty built after the first three. These had bigger tank and bunker, taller chimneys and domes and some frame strengthening. Photograph F.H. Stingemore, The Transport Treasury.

Slightly ethereally through that slow film of so long ago, one of the original three locos of 1927, 4998, stands at Cricklewood. The first three got the freight loco LMS panel on the cabside but this was not repeated on the others. Note the main differences from 4970; lower chimney and dome, tender sides, lower tank. Later 4998 got a coal rail to the tender top, in lieu it would seem, of the rotary bunker it never got. Photograph F.H. Stingemore, The Transport Treasury.

Glorious picture of an unknown Garratt (such is the grime on the side) ploughing its way up to London on the Midland, on the Up Slow just south of Radlett. The later thirty, and 4997, got the rotary bunkers in 1932-33, leaving 4998 and 4999 with straight bunkers to the end of their lives. Renumbering of the whole series of thirty-three from 4967-4999 to 7967-7999 took place in 1938. The loco here is in the 'preferred way round' – that is, bunker at rear. It was great good fortune that Cricklewood had the famous 'East-West Loop' which allowed them to run under the main line and turn for the journey back north – as in the two photos opposite. Presumably a nearby triangle sufficed for the same purpose at Toton. Photograph The Transport Treasury.

47999, one of the two (of three) originals which kept the straight bunker – just south of Leicester at a guess, about to diverge on to the Burton line at Knighton North Junction (now built over). The original three were vacuum fitted for operating the steam brake. This was a typical duty for the two straight bunker engines, more 'local' in nature to stem Firemen's objection to burrowing into the coal supply. Photograph Canon George, The Transport Treasury.

Riley's Railway Roundabout
Either Side of Caerphilly, 12 May 1952
6423

Left and above. Riley's Railway Roundabout is a favourite feature in our parent magazine, *British Railways Illustrated* – an unparalleled photographic record of Britain's railways 'south of a line from Birmingham to the Wash'. From Saturday 10 May to the following Saturday, 17 May 1952, our intrepid photographer spent the days investigating some of the Valley lines accessible from Cardiff. Big wheeled Cathays pannier tank 6423 was chimney first 'up into the hills' (in typical Valleys fashion) when viewed from Station Terrace, Penyrheol with an up train for Senghenydd on 12 May 1952. The formation here was made for double track, as was the bridge on which the photographer is standing, but it never took place. Photographs R.C. Riley, The Transport Treasury.

With its motley stock, 6423 is now at the south end of its train ready to return to Caerphilly. The leading coach is ex-Taff Vale trailer 4023 (steam railcar 14 of 1906) provided as 'workmen's' accommodation. The other two vehicles are ex-Cardiff Railway auto-cars 143 and 144. The remains of Universal Colliery are in the background. Photographs R.C. Riley, The Transport Treasury.

On the same day 0-6-2T 6603, another Cathays engine, enters Senghenydd down platform loop with a typical 'time capsule' of colliers' stock, this time some ancient rattling four wheelers. Coal was everywhere on the Valley lines of course and a system of almost informal workings (many began to appear in the public timetables under BR) served the needs of miners and their shifts up and down the lines. This is the Llanbradach colliers' train, which had run since 1941. Photograph R.C. Riley, The Transport Treasury.

The Senghenydd branch joined the Rhymney Railway's 'main line' at Aber Junction and branch trains continued to Caerphilly or beyond. On the far side of the town, at the other end of the lengthy Caerphilly tunnel and just beyond Cefn On station, were the sidings and wagon works at Cherry Orchard. The sidings dated from a 1912 scheme which also involved the quadrupling of the tracks and indeed the opening of Cefn On station in 1915. One of the enduring features of South Wales freight train working was 'the engine and brake' which, were it anywhere else, would be a simple light engine – they did not like to be parted! This is Rhymney Railway 0-6-2T 35 of Cardiff East Dock, leaving the sidings with the inevitable brake and heading south on 12 May 1952. Photograph R.C. Riley, The Transport Treasury.

Above and below. Two contrasting trains at Cherry Orchard that day. Above, a sprightly 2-6-2T, 4143 of Rhymney, heads north past the sidings with the 4.48pm Cardiff Bute Street-Rhymney train. The difference in levels of the up line on which the train is travelling and the down, on top of the bank, is one outcome of the new work of 1912-15. Taff Vale 0-6-2T 390 is at the head of a down 'Caerphilly works train' for staff at the extensive works there. Photograph R.C. Riley, The Transport Treasury.

Above and below. Ex-Rhymney Railway 0-6-2Ts 77 and 78 on consecutive up passenger trains pass Cherry Orchard, one after the other in convenient numerical sequence, 12 May 1952. Target letters/numbers in South Wales usually started at the beginning of the day in order but as it progressed of course they got more and more mixed up. Those with an eye for detail will note the large BR crest on the first one's tank and the smaller version on the second. Photographs R.C. Riley, The Transport Treasury.

Above and below. A little later, Target RL passes on an up train (above) behind a less-than steam tight Rhymney 0-6-2T 5674; the five coach set includes a fine clerestory vehicle behind the engine. Below, yet another Rhymney 0-6-2T, 5603, comes south with a down train, another five coach rake of which at least four are moderately respectable. Note that odd piece of gadgetry which lifts the point rodding to the higher level. Photographs R.C. Riley, The Transport Treasury. *Additional notes and information by Bryan Wilson.*

Edinburgh Waverley was unique. Not only did it witness the cream of East Coast steam traction for nearly half a century, but the setting, both natural and man made, was incomparable. Prior to Grouping, North British or North Eastern Atlantics, together with the latest 4-4-0s, hauled most principal trains north to Aberdeen and south to Newcastle. Then came the memorable Gresley era, beginning with the A1 Pacifics which evolved into A3s. A landmark was the introduction of the non-stop summer 'Flying Scotsman' from Waverley to Kings Cross. Another notable development was the advent of mighty P2 2-8-2s for the Aberdeen road. Even more excitement was generated by the streamlined A4s and the high-speed 'Coronation'. After Gresley's death, the motley collection of Thompson A2 Pacifics emerged, followed by Peppercorn's version, then his highly competent A1s. For many years, Edinburgh Haymarket shed turned out most of its engines, especially top link Pacifics, in immaculate mechanical and external condition, thus adding gloss to the glamour.

Despite its size, Waverley was far from a cathedral of the railway age. Its low site and strict limitations on the height of structures above track level saw to that. Nevertheless, the North British managed to provide some high quality architecture within these restrictions when the station was rebuilt at the end of the nineteenth century. The North British Hotel was a different matter, a huge Edwardian pile at the east end of Princes Street and a prominent feature of the Edinburgh skyline, even from the Forth Bridge approach viaduct eight miles away. Other noble edifices peering down on the railway were the defiant walls of the castle and the dour ramparts of Calton Gaol, west and east of Waverley respectively. Such lofty perches were made possible by hills of resilient rock, the cores of ancient volcanoes. Along with Princes Street, its associated gardens, the Scott Monument and The Mound, they gave the centre of Edinburgh its character. In this setting, the railway was bound to be something special.

Information on the engines in these illustrations has been gleaned from *Locomotives of the LNER*, an all-time epic of railway research by the RCTS. More *Waverley Wonders* from Irwell Press are imminent – wait for it to burst upon us in 2003.

Waverley W

By Paul Anderson

Right. A4 60031 GOLDEN PLOVER poses magnificently at the west end of Waverley, probably with a Glasgow Queen Street train. Although the photograph is not dated, it was most likely taken in 1956-57. The leading Gresley coach is still in fairly glossy 'blood and custard', while the Edinburgh Corporation bus crossing Waverley Bridge is one of the large fleet purchased to replace the trams in 1955-56. In the right background is the lower part of the medieval Old Town with its Victorian accretions. GOLDEN PLOVER was shedded at Haymarket from October 1937 to May 1962 and in the spring of 1939 had no less than 39 consecutive round trips on the non-stop 'Coronation' to and from Kings Cross. Photograph The Transport Treasury.

Clearly this was a chance shot, but even behind a fence A4 4483 KINGFISHER looks impressive. Unfortunately, this only applies to the sleek streamlining. It is early summer 1937 and the Gresley Pacific wore that unsatisfactory livery whereby the whole smokebox was painted black and this ended in a vertical division with the apple green boiler cladding. Subsequent liveries employed the familiar parabolic curve. The Glasgow Queen Street train is at platform 14. KINGFISHER was the first of the class at Haymarket shed, arriving in December 1936, and apart from short spells at Kings Cross and Doncaster, stayed there until September 1963. As 60024, this was the last A4 to work a scheduled passenger train, the 8.25am from Glasgow Buchanan Street to Aberdeen on 14 September 1966. Photograph Dr R.A. Read, Gavin Whitelaw Collection.

ders

With a neat touch of symmetry, Mound Tunnel was mirrored at the east end of Waverley by Calton Tunnel. Both were built for double track, but the increase in capacity necessitated by the opening of the Forth Bridge meant that four sets of rails had to be accommodated. In the case of Calton Tunnel, a second double-track bore was drilled in the 1890s, thus the sign 'Calton North Tunnel length 475 Yards'. In marked contrast to the verdant canopy of Princes Street Gardens, rugged crags on the side of Calton Hill dominated this approach to the station. Star of the show in this 29 August 1953 view is J83 68474, one of the fully-lined east end pilots kept beautifully clean by St Margarets shed. The engine entered service in April 1901 and was withdrawn in April 1958. Photograph John Robertson, The Transport Treasury.

Top right. A somewhat unusual view of the east end of Waverley on 19 September 1949, showing A3 60094 COLORADO waiting at platform 20 with a southbound express. The lengthy island platform on the south side of the station, outside the overall roof, was primarily intended for suburban services, although it sometimes handled main line traffic, especially at busy times. From this angle, the fine stonework and transverse roof gables dating from the reconstruction of the station in 1892-1900 are prominent, albeit overshadowed by St Andrews House on the site of Calton Gaol. COLORADO was at Haymarket from December 1947 to December 1961 after a long period at Carlisle, where it worked into Edinburgh over the Waverley route. The Pacific spent some time at St Rollox on Glasgow - Perth - Aberdeen expresses prior to withdrawal in February 1964. Photograph Dr D.M. Alexander, The Transport Treasury.

Below. It was worth ascending the Scott Monument, as the view of Waverley in its setting was even more breathtaking than the climb. In the background is the Old Town, with the Church of Scotland Assembly Hall prominent. On the right are The Mound and the National Gallery of Scotland. In the foreground, Princes Street Gardens drop down to the railway. On 23 September 1963, A3 60057 ORMONDE and a Derby Type 4 diesel arrive from the west. The latter will take over a Waverley route train, While the St Margarets Pacific is rostered for the 3.43pm to Berwick. After over 38 years service, 60057 is nearing the end of its career and was withdrawn the following month. Although the engine spent about half its life at Haymarket, it did have a spell at St Margarets in 1939-40 for working the Waverley route. Photograph The Transport Treasury.

Below right. The western approach to Waverley provided a particularly attractive and popular setting for photographs of railway activity in Edinburgh. With the foliage of Princes Street Gardens and the noble portal of Mound Tunnel as a backdrop, A2 60532 BLUE PETER backs down from Haymarket shed on 4 July 1959 to take over an Aberdeen express. The Pacific went new to York in March 1948 and moved to Haymarket during November 1949. In common with several other members of the class, it would probably have spent the bulk of its career there. However, Aberdeen shed regarded single chimney A2s as poor steamers and managed to exchange one of them, 60537 BACHELORS BUTTON, with BLUE PETER in January 1951. Haymarket did not discriminate between the two versions and, in any case, had a knack of getting any engine to perform properly. 60532 moved from Aberdeen to Dundee in June 1961 and was withdrawn at the end of 1966, prior to preservation. Photograph John Robertson, The Transport Treasury.

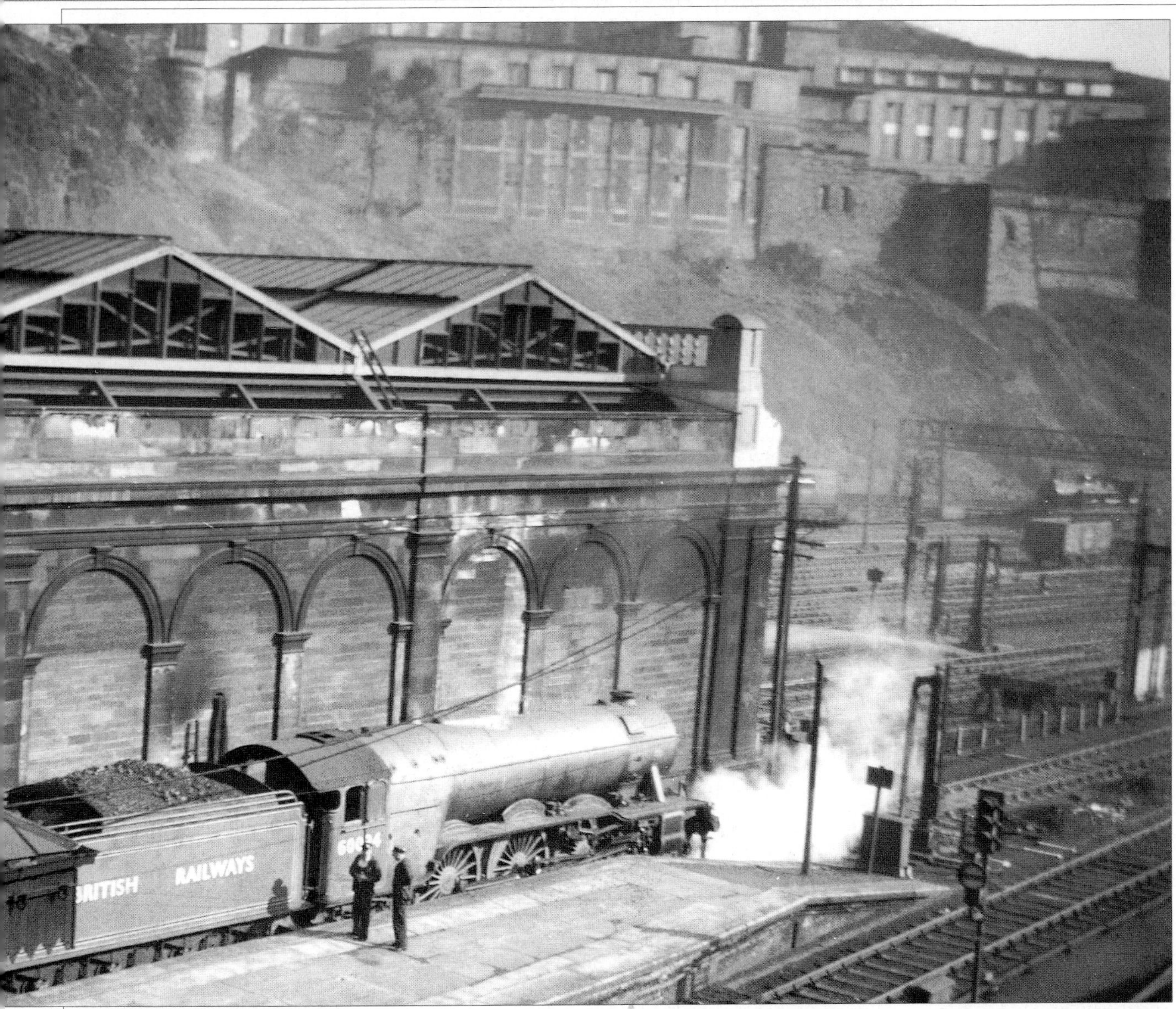
BRITISH RAILWAYS

60532
BLUE PETER
60532
15

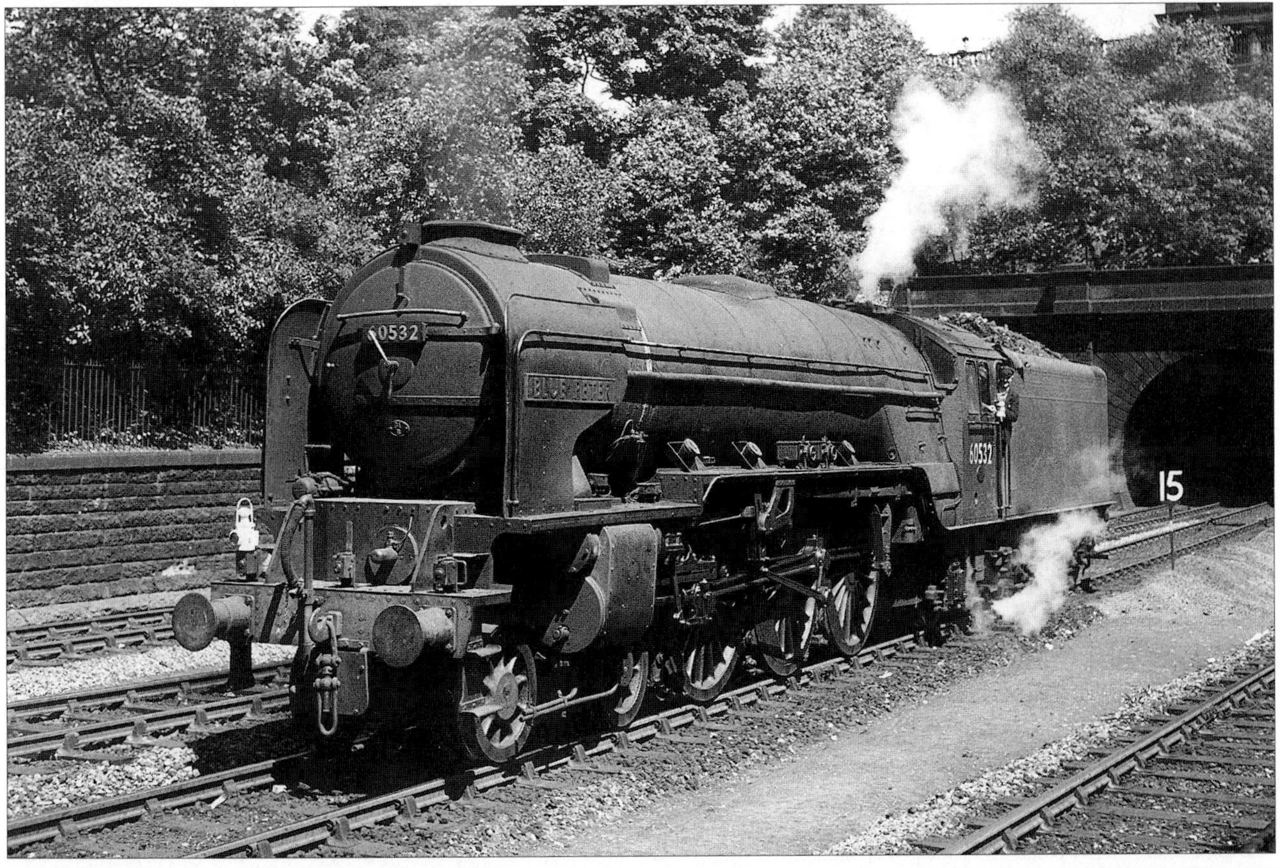

Notes by John Talbot

Melmerby was prominent even in a district where there were twenty-two junctions within a radius of fifteen miles. These two views, probably (like the others)taken in 1961 or 1962, are north from Melmerby North signal box. The Tanfield branch diverges left and the Thirsk line on the right has been lifted after its closure on 14 September 1959. Along the Northallerton line, between the two branches, there were medium sized nineteenth century signalboxes at each end of the station. The northern one stood near the two huts by the barrow crossing in the middle distance, and controlled the original junction to Masham which was at that site. In 1912 or 1913 (reliable documents differ) the box at the level crossing (from which these views were taken) was about doubled in length (at its south end) and the Down platform and the Masham junction were transposed to their new positions shown, leaving only the one signalbox. The fenced path on the left is an interesting alternative to a footbridge for linking the platforms, though a very unusual footbridge is shown there as well, in photographs dated 1949. Almost invisible beyond the far platform is a second crossover which was retained until the final closure of Melmerby. This was to run-round the engine of the early-morning 'Ripon Mail' which came through to here from Leeds to save manning Ripon box at that time of day – awkward for signalmen's rosters. Photographs The Transport Treasury.

MELMERBY

The view southwards, showing the enlarged signal box. This had a frame of 64 levers including two gate-wheels, separated by a plate between them, for the signalman to stand on. The plate was the equivalent of about five levers, making the interlocking frame of a length for 69 levers. This made it, in early BR days, the largest Harrogate District Frame. The large patch of fresh ballast is the site of the Thirsk lines junction. Old railwaymen of the district often called this the 'Thirsk Road', perhaps a 150 year old title from the days when railways were in a rudimentary form, replacing stage coaches. This passed through a separate level crossing (hence the two gate wheels mentioned earlier) which is seen being dismantled by men using the ex-GC mess and tool van in the goods yard. At the end of the signal box the steps include a wooden 'tablet-stand' for the signalman to exchange the Masham branch single-line authority. The little Down Siding in the distance had an interesting history. Originally it connected near the tablet-stand (hence the vacant space by the Down line). During World War 2 it was extended to motorised points 860 yards south of the box, creating a loop which was one of many World War II enhancements in the Harrogate District. So that trains from the loop could go to Thirsk as well as to the other two lines, the siding connection was also moved south as shown. Although the entry to the loop was abolished after 1945, the siding remained until 1965 to give access to the coal depots via a line well behind the signal box. The Second World War alterations, involving the Down line only, made for a curious signalling part-anachronism inside the box. Levers for the Up signals remained arranged in the NER fashion (whereby the Distant signal levers were between the end of the frame and their Stop signal levers). Levers for the Down signals were rearranged in the LNER fashion (whereby Distant signal levers were towards the centre of the frame from their stop signal levers) to give slightly easier 'consequential pulling sequences'. A comparable part-anachronism existed in the signal box at Ripon where the Up Siding was likewise converted into a Second World War loop, with Up signal levers re-arranged in the LNER fashion whereas the Down levers remained in the NER fashion. Photographs The Transport Treasury.

This view combines the others and shows more of the abolished Thirsk Road level crossing. The small buildings behind the signal box were used to store redundant equipment – worth a visit! There were a few 'near-miss' accidents here. Much earlier on, the nearer signal in the first two photographs was a bracket with another arm for the converging Thirsk Road. On one occasion a test-train ('TT' ex-Darlington) was admitted up to this signal. The signalman then wound both gates to allow a preceding train from Thirsk to be followed immediately by the 'TT'. Unfortunately the 'TT' driver took the wrong arm as his and started off, into a sideways 'nudge' with the other train on the junction. This caused the habit of bracketing converging signals to be changed to one of spreading them out onto well separated posts. The locomotive of the 'TT' was remembered as being the 4-6-4 'Hush-Hush' engine No.10000. 'TT's often did a 'standing-start' at the bottom of the 3 mile 1 in 133 bank near Littlethorpe box, south of Ripon, hence the need to regulate them at Melmerby or Ripon behind trains not making the same stop. Incidentally the 4-6-4 wheelbase of the 'W1' was too rigid for many crossovers and siding points, so signalmen all over Yorkshire were rather wary of shunting it. On another occasion some new electric track-circuits were installed on the Down. An early train bound for Thirsk approached in darkness. The signalman plainly wound the Northallerton line gates instead. Finding his signal lever locked normal he believed the 'new-fangled' devices had failed, instead of the frame's usual interlocking holding the lever. All too quickly he went down onto the tablet-stand and gave a green lamp handsignal to the driver, who then proceeded to completely run through and demolish the unopened Thirsk line gates. Not shown in these photographs was a completely new Second World War signalbox 1 mile 53 yards south of Melmerby. This caused the box at the level crossing to be renamed Melmerby North whilst the new box was Melmerby South. It controlled a triangular junction to Royal Ordnance Factory Stores commonly known as the Dump. The north-east side of the triangle did not last long, the main-line points being lifted out by steam crane on 18 September 1955 and the consequential signalling alterations were made during the following week. The eastern junction points were, however, handed over to the local permanent-way staff with instructions to re-use them to create a new 'end-dock' further inside the Dump. These points were of the 'Wye' type, i.e. both tracks as they diverged were curved instead of one being straight. The job was duly done and it turned out the new dock was specially built for an important trial of loading caterpillar-tracked army vehicles (of a new type) onto flat railway wagons as fast as possible. When the 'top-brass' (both military and railway) were assembled the trial began. All went well until the vehicles, speeding along the wagon tops, reached the point where the train was curved and most of them, like dominoes, fell off sideways as their caterpillar-tracks' steering was not refined enough to cope with the exact radius of the curve. Incidentally the new signal box was built slightly longer than necessary to allow the branches to the Dump to be double instead of single tracks, but this extra outdoor work was never done. In its latter days the box was manned by one of the North box men walking out to it, until it was replaced by a Ground Frame on 24 August 1966. This just worked the south-east curve connection with the Up Main. Ordinarily it should have been released by Melmerby North, but in fact was locked by a key kept at Ripon – a rather unusual arrangement. The box at the station level crossing then became, again, the only box at Melmerby. It was a place of happy memories – for most people. Photographs The Transport Treasury.

Two Guises of the 'Turbo'

'The Turbomotive' 6202, in different guises officially recorded by the LMS. The differences are the boiler. From *The Book of the Princess Royal Pacifics* by Ian Sixsmith (Irwell Press, 2000): *'The first boiler was similar to those of the second batch of ten Princesses; in fact the first of the boilers intended for the ten, with 32 superheater element, was 'diverted' to the turbine project. The regulator was combined in the superheater header. Of two spare boilers built one, with 40 superheater elements, replaced the 'Turbo's' first boiler, in July 1936 – this had a dome to house the regulator. The Turbomotive was out of action for such protracted periods that this boiler, No.9236, could be used on other Princesses in the meantime!'* Top, with 'domeless' boiler, she is pristine; note the casing covering the atomiser steam supply – absent once reboilered – just behind the chimney spanning smokebox and boiler cladding. The lining goes over it – the 'boundary' between the black and red livery! Below, 6202 (now a little travel-worn) has the 'domed' boiler. Note the new hinged circular inspection cover on the casing just forward of the cab as well as smaller one to its right, with evidence of touched-up paintwork. That is presumably an early speedo drive leading from the centre of the trailing driving axle to the cab.

DIESEL DAWN Unwelcome Visitors

As is well known the first years of main line diesel running on BR were notable for the unfortunate way the new traction was simply plonked down amidst the steam fleet it would replace at sheds all over the country. The deleterious effects were known but there was little that could be done – provision of proper depots had to be hurried along to catch up with the growing numbers of the incomers. Still it made for some fine sights, such as 10001 at Willesden and D604 COSSACK a short distance away on Old Oak shed, on the same day in September 1960. Photograph A.F. Cottrell, The Transport Treasury.

Some early Peaks among the steam locos at Upperby. The date is unknown, but it would be the period after their building in 1959 to 1961 or thereabouts, when they worked on the West Coast main line. The Jubilee on the left is 45588 KASHMIR. Photograph The Transport Treasury.

A big main line diesel at a very different shed, D1052 WESTERN VICEROY then only a few months old, at Severn Tunnel Junction on 3 July 1963. Diesels had increasingly usurped the shed by now and it only had a couple of years to go before closure. The concrete supports would be relics of the 1947 oil burning fiasco. Photograph A.F. Cottrell, The Transport Treasury.

TILBURY

Notes by Bryan Wilson

Looking west through the main circulating area after the LMS reconstruction. The 'Way Out' is for local passengers. It is Coronation time, 1953, with the bunting on display. The directing sign to the Post Office on top of the letter box, the vintage stamp machines on the Ticket Office wall and posters for 'Craven A' plus 'Season Tickets for Juveniles' are all tiny fragments of our rich railway and social history.

> **'In this vicinity there was an ancient ferry across the Thames, said to be the place where Claudius passed in pursuit of the Britons'.**

1. THE RAILWAY COMPANIES

The London Tilbury & Southend Extension Railway reached Tilbury at a station near the Fort on 13 April 1854. It ran from a connection with the Eastern Counties Railway at Forest Gate Junction, via Barking. The 'Fort' at Tilbury was named after one of Henry VIII's blockhouses. Later in 1854, on 14 August, a connection was made to Stanford Le Hope, then on to Pitsea, reached on 1 July 1855. The 'third side' of the Tilbury triangle (Tilbury North Curve) also dates from about 1855.

In 1882, a 'Tilbury & Gravesend Tunnel Junction' Railway was sanctioned but capital was not attracted and Powers were abandoned in 1885. Likewise, a Romford-Tilbury line, planned to break the LT&S monopoly, was defeated in the Lords.

The 'Direct' line from Barking via Upminster to Pitsea was opened throughout on 1 June 1888 and apart from its latter-day use by commuters, was a means of easing the pressure on the Barking-Tilbury line, thus allowing it to cope with the increasing traffic on that route.

The Tottenham & Forest Gate Railway opened from South Tottenham to Forest Gate Junction on 9 July 1894 (2 July for goods) thus allowing the Midland Railway to reach Tilbury. The Midland duly absorbed the LT&S on 1 January 1912; the Act for the take-over was actually dated 7 August that year, but was legally backdated to 1 January.

The Midland of course became part of the LMS in 1923 and ultimately the London Midland Region of a nationalised BR. The Tilbury section reverted to the Eastern Region, arguably its rightful place, on 20 February 1949.

2. THE STATIONS

'Riverside'

The original Tilbury station was small, constructed of timber and duly became inadequate. Reconstruction was undertaken between 1906 and 1908 and whilst this upgrading provided a large covered circulating area for passengers, extensive office accommodation and refreshment rooms, travellers still joined or disembarked from ships in the Docks, or were 'shuttled' by the ferry steamers to or from their ships which anchored in Gravesend Reach.

When agreement was reached in 1921 between the Port of London Authority – which controlled Tilbury Docks – and the Midland Railway, to provide a new Landing Stage at Riverside, it was not possible to attach it to the existing scheme of things so once more, the station facilities were reconstructed. This work included the provision of a baggage examination hall, alongside and connecting with the station, for the use of the Customs authorities.

On 16 May 1930 the new floating landing stage was opened by Prime Minister J. Ramsay Macdonald and from that time on was used by liners calling to land or embark passengers. The floating landing stage was 1,142 feet long; the LMS had 300 feet at the east end for Gravesend ferry traffic and the remainder was for the use or the liners. The station was arranged as an 'integrated unit' with buildings designed by the LMS Chief Engineer. There were four passenger platforms, each over 800ft long plus two more platforms for baggage. There was a large

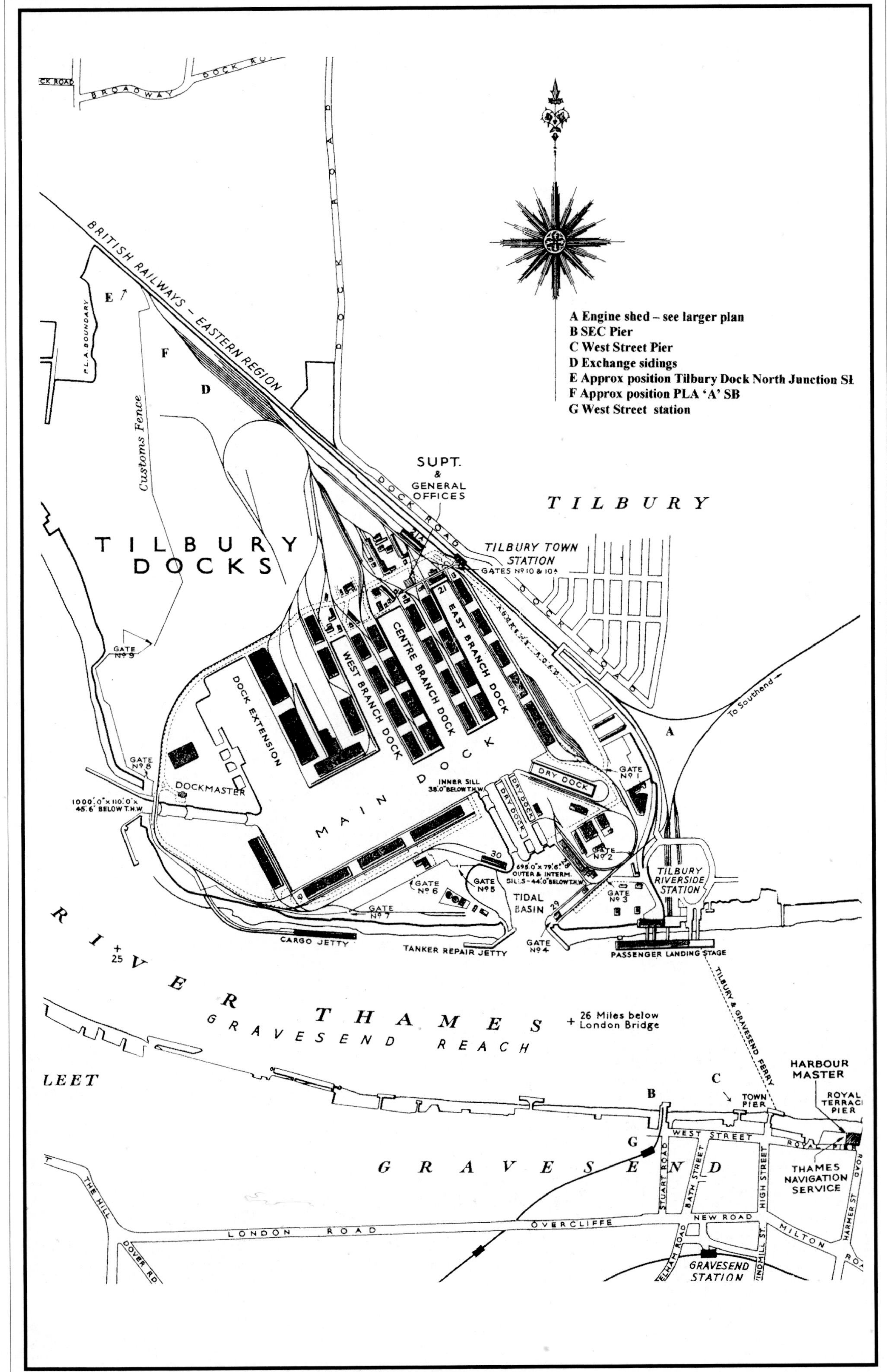
A Engine shed – see larger plan
B SEC Pier
C West Street Pier
D Exchange sidings
E Approx position Tilbury Dock North Junction SB
F Approx position PLA 'A' SB
G West Street station
TILBURY DOCKS
TILBURY
BRITISH RAILWAYS – EASTERN REGION
SUPT. & GENERAL OFFICES
TILBURY TOWN STATION
GATES Nº 10 & 10A
DOCK ROAD
Customs Fence
P.L.A. BOUNDARY
DOCK EXTENSION
WEST BRANCH DOCK
CENTRE BRANCH DOCK
EAST BRANCH DOCK
MAIN DOCK
DRY DOCK
DOCKMASTER
INNER SILL 38.0" BELOW T.H.W.
1000.0" x 110.0" x 45.6" BELOW T.H.W.
695.0" x 79.6" OUTER & INTERM. SILLS - 44.0" BELOW T.H.W.
TIDAL BASIN
TILBURY RIVERSIDE STATION
To Southend
GATE Nº 1
GATE Nº 2
GATE Nº 3
GATE Nº 4
GATE Nº 5
GATE Nº 6
GATE Nº 7
GATE Nº 8
GATE Nº 9
CARGO JETTY
TANKER REPAIR JETTY
PASSENGER LANDING STAGE
TILBURY & GRAVESEND FERRY
RIVER THAMES
GRAVESEND REACH
26 Miles below London Bridge
HARBOUR MASTER
TOWN PIER
ROYAL TERRACE PIER
THAMES NAVIGATION SERVICE
WEST STREET
STUART ROAD
BATH STREET
HIGH STREET
NEW ROAD
LONDON ROAD
OVERCLIFFE
MILTON
HARMER ST
THE HILL
DOVER RD
GRAVESEND STATION
GRAVESEND
BROADWAY
DOCK ROAD

concourse area adjacent to the customs hall. The station was wholly LMS-owned and completely independent of the Port of London Authority (PLA) facilities.

In 1935, Tilbury station became 'Tilbury Riverside', first appearing as such in the timetable dated 6 July 1936. Thus it remained until closure after the last normal service on 28 November 1992. After this date, a bus sufficed from Tilbury Town, with through ticketing. At the time of closure, Riverside station was described as 'a listed building in poor condition'.

Tilbury Town (originally Tilbury Docks)

Tilbury Docks station opened for a workmen's service from Grays about May 1884 and was part of the agreement between the Dock company and the LTSR in November 1883 to provide such a station. It opened for public use on the same day as the Dock, 17 April 1886 – in that year the area was described as 'a sprawling settlement where the first houses for the Dock workers were built'. Previously, the only traffic had been in connection with the Gravesend ferry.

Docks station became 'Tilbury Town for Tilbury Docks' officially from 3 August 1934 and in the public notices from 1 October 1934.

Tilbury Marine

This 'station' consisted of a single platform adjoining No.29 Shed in the Docks. It was used in connection with LMS and 'ALA' (NORD) steamers to the Continent via Dunkirk. It opened in May 1927 and only lasted until 1 May 1932, the last sailing from Tilbury being the 11.30pm departure the previous night. ALA then operated out of Folkestone.

The station had a timber booking office, first class accommodation, plus other facilities. The railway company hired the booking office from the PLA and issued tickets for both inland and overseas destinations. Access to the main line was from Tilbury South Junction.

Tidal Basin

Nos.28 and 29 Berths were laid out as a passenger station when the Dock opened. Known as 'Tidal Basin' station, there was direct rail connection to the main line from Tilbury West Junction – it is not marked on the plan but its approximate position was a little to the west of 'Gate No.3'. The direct connection was removed by 1913, enabling an overbridge to be built for the diverted Ferry Road. A connection was restored in April 1927, from the South Junction for Tilbury Marine station (see previous paragraph). Ferry Road was originally a level thoroughfare across the front of the station and passengers walked across it between ferry and train.

3. TRAIN SERVICES

In the 1863 'Bradshaw' there were ten trains each weekday from London to Tilbury, of which six continued to and from Southend. Best times were 40 minutes from London and 43 minutes on return. By 1910, towards the end of the LT&S regime, this had risen to 26 each way. By then, it was 43 minutes down and 50 minutes back.

In 1953 over 600 liners, requiring 571 special trains, berthed at Riverside landing stage. Such specials had a preponderance of first class stock, as befitted the well-heeled liner custom. They bore carriage nameboards such as 'Orient Line', 'Swedish Lloyd' and so on. The trains loaded up to ten passenger vehicles plus a couple of luggage vans. Swedish Lloyd operated a Tilbury-Gothenburg service and Tilbury became the British base for Peninsular & Oriental and Orient Lines with services to Australia via India and Singapore, and to the Far East generally.

The platform entrances with their 'concertina' gates. The 'Buffet and Dining Room' and Cooks Bureau de Change give the place a 'Continental' air; the vintage newspaper trolley of W.H. Smith's outside the Platform 3 entrance completes the scene.

Left. **By 20 March 1956 the letter box has displaced the stamp machines which have moved in turn to the corner of the Booking Office. Not much going on but someone from Headquarters has decided on 'improvements'. The previously clear Platform numbers high up on the gates have been replaced by small enamel signs sticking out from the wall. The kiosk has gone upmarket to 'Tobacco and Confectionery' and the Ladies has First and Third Class waiting facilities. One of the posters invites us to sample Carlisle.**

Tickets, mostly first class of course, could be obtained on the ship after berthing and from an improvised booking office on the Quayside. In those days, takings of £300 for a London train were considered very satisfactory. At that time the total station staff at Riverside, made up of Inspectors, Guards, Signalmen, Porter, Shunters and Clerks, was 120.

The boat trains generally ran to and from St Pancras where facilities for passengers and luggage were superior to those at Fenchurch Street. In 1955 500 liners still called with the same number of boat trains required, conveying nearly 150,000 passengers. In the same year, nearly a million tickets were sold at Riverside to local passengers. The best the local service could provide at this time was 41 minutes from Fenchurch Street (22 miles).

In 1963, just thirty special boat trains ran. Prior to this, there were also 'ordinary' trains of LMS compartment stock with 2-6-4Ts running from Fenchurch Street, mainly to serve Russian Cruise liners at the Landing Stage. Electrification of the LTS came in June 1962, after being first promised in 1912 and again in 1950. This meant EMU stock was used from 1963 from Fenchurch Street, guaranteeing the loss of any 'quality' traffic. The liners anyway by this date were relocating to Southampton.

From 1983, Tilbury Town was served only by two trains an hour from Fenchurch Street to Southend the 'long way round', missing

Looking out to the River, in Coronation year. The sign for the Gravesend Ferry can be seen through the arch. The 'Bureau de Change' direction board still reflects the nature of the place. A poster in this view tells of the 'fog' service from Fenchurch Street – planned reductions were a regular winter feature during London 'smogs' – and there are crowd control barriers handy for 'when the boat comes in'.

Riverside, leaving that imposing terminal to be served hourly only from Upminster. As mentioned, all services to Riverside ceased towards the end of 1992.

Finally a mention must be made that, in busier times at least, one Boat Train per week passed over the PLA system to the Quays, under 'One Train working' regulations from the Exchange Sidings near Tilbury Town station.

4. DOCKS

In the early years of the 19th Century, the East and West India Docks were opened in East London. Individual companies owned each Dock but as the century progressed they started to merge. One to emerge thus was 'The East & West India Docks Company'. Saddled with the earliest docks of 1802 and 1806 which badly needed modernisation, together with the threat offered by the opening of the new Albert Dock in 1880, the company was faced with a gloomy choice. Either it modernised their ancient docks and lost traffic while it did so (the job would take up to three years) or it lost business to those who did. The Directors decided to construct new docks at Tilbury to intercept traffic from the upstream docks, also to save shipping time and the associated expense. Plans had in fact been deposited for a dock at Tilbury as far back as the 1865 Session of Parliament, but they did not materialise. Indeed. the E & W India Dock Co's engineer (A. Manning) in his earlier career had produced another scheme in 1867 – but again nothing came of it.

For the reasons outlined above, in 1881 the Secretary of the E & W India Dock Co supported Mr Manning, and in the competitive era in which they operated, land 'was obtained by secret agents before the scheme became public'. The necessary Act was duly obtained on 3 July 1882 with the 'first turf' being cut just five days later. More than fifty acres of water were initially impounded, later increasing to 104 acres.

Dissension on the LTS Board meant that other items associated with the new Dock were not formalised until an Agreement of November 1883. These briefly were:-

(a) LTS to build a new station to be called 'Tilbury Dock'.

(b) A connection to be installed with the Dock railway system – at what became Tilbury Dock North Junction.

(c) Stipulations regarding the passenger train service.

(d) The LTS were to provide a London goods depot for Tilbury docks traffic at Commercial Road. Special freight rates applied for dock traffic as there were insufficient warehouses in the new docks and the traffic needed to reach London without delay.

e) Special trains were to be run as required in connection with the ships.

The Dock contractors were Messrs Kirk & Randall but they were soon in difficulties and work stopped for a while. A new contract went to Lucas & Aird in October 1884. The estimated £1.1m for the work reached a frightening £2.8m by the time of completion. Low estimates to encourage support, and cost overruns when realities have to be faced are nothing new.

The wider view eastwards, 20 March 1956. The only place doing any business is the bookstall but Riverside was like that, long periods of inactivity punctuated by periods of frantic activity. A partially-obscured 'Swedish Lloyd' sign with a slot to insert the destination board can be seen below the Platform 4 sign.

The Dock opened on 17 April 1886 and the same day the North End Exchange Sidings come into use. There was no business during the first four months except for one line of German steamers. In August the same year, Clan Line, who planned to use the new Albert Dock, were persuaded to go to Tilbury with the inducement of a 10 year agreement at half rates. The Anchor Line, Atlantic Transport Line, Orient Line and three smaller companions followed, all getting reduced rates for a number of years. The Dock did, however, eventually kill what little general cargo was formerly dealt with at Thames Haven. Despite all this the East & West India Dock

The Coronation-bedecked covered footpath to the Gravesend Ferry at the Landing Stage. The board facing us at the end is hard to read but it looks like 'Next Ferry for Gravesend'. A lone member of staff awaits business between the usual 'fits and starts'.

Co earnings for 1887 did not cover working expenses and they were bankrupt in 1888 with a Receiver appointed. The competitive struggle ended in March 1888 with a 'Working Agreement' between the London & St Katharines Docks Company and the East & West India Dock Co, who later amalgamated to become the London & India Docks Company on New Years Day 1901.

Following a Royal Commission Report, the 'Port of London' Act was passed in 1908 which transferred the Dock companies to the Port of London Authority as from 1 January 1909. It covered all the companies below Teddington on the River Thames. Nothing had been done at Tilbury since opening in 1886, and improvements elsewhere caused shipowners to move their vessels. Seeing this happen, in 1917 the PLA extended the length of the main dock to 1,450ft.

In 1921 a new cargo jetty was built out in the river itself in the Gravesend Reach to accommodate ships requiring to unload part of their cargo before proceeding upriver. This jetty was 1,000ft long and 80ft wide, parallel to and 160 feet from the north bank of the river with two berths for passenger and cargo liners and a curved viaduct approach. Ever larger vessels dictated that a new access lock to the main docks be provided in 1929. This gave direct access to the western end of the main dock. A new passenger landing stage was opened in 1930 and during the Second World War traffic increased to levels never before experienced. In the 1950s further work took place, involving the widening of the western part of the main dock and

All aboard! Genuine 1950s apparel with flat caps and natty hats. The sign at the end of the walkway says 'Spitting Prohibited' – TB was still a threat to public health. The extent of the station building – pure LMS in style – is clear in this view. The landing stage sits on 63 steel pontoons, moored by chain cables and steel girders to the shore. It rises and falls with the tide as do the connecting gangways for passengers. The total weight is about 400 tons and there is a separate vehicular bridge for the passage of motor vehicles and so on.

The River, 20 March 1956, as the ferry takes its leave. This was a time when Londoners believed, with a sort of inverted pride, that anyone falling in the Thames would be poisoned before they could drown. All the impedimenta of 'ship to shore' operations are here and the access to the station circulating area is clearly seen with bridges for inward and outward traffic. The left-hand building is the PLA customs and baggage hall.

the building of a new quay known as No.1 Berth. A new 'T' shaped transit shed with road and rail facilities was completed in June 1957.

In the early years, the only freight traffic was local As part of the November 1883 'Agreement', the LTS was required to construct a junction with the Dock Railways at Tilbury Dock North Junction, and the Dock Company to provide Exchange Sidings. These Exchange sidings materialised as three sets of sidings:

Outwards Section 220 wagon capacity.

Reception (Inwards) Section 120 wagon capacity.

Marshalling Section 220 wagon capacity.

The Marshalling Section was used to form vehicles in the correct order for the Dock Area. Three additional sidings were for surplus empty wagons and so on. There was also a connection at the South Junction end used only between 6pm and 6am when North Junction Box was closed. PLA signal box 'A', located at the west end of the Exchange Sidings, worked direct to Tilbury Town North Junction box. It is interesting that in the Exchange Sidings, LTS locomotives could take water but it had to be 'paid for', a ticket being issued which then passed into the accounts system.

There were fifty miles of PLA railway within the Docks including facilities at the front and rear of every berth. Until 1939 there was no road access and 87% of Dock traffic was railborne. By 1959 this was down to 35% and two years later forwardings had fallen to 250 loaded wagons daily. Added to this, there were 17,000 consignments of 'Passengers' Luggage in Advance' for the Liner traffic. From 25 July 1969, all rail traffic for general cargo berths ceased and the freight facilities were transformed into the 'London Container Terminal' at Tilbury, which in fact consisted of two Freightliner Terminals and a rail-connected grain terminal.

Commercial Road Depot

Although it was in London, rather than Tilbury, Commercial Road Depot was linked directly with the latter both in construction and operation. As we have seen, the provision of the Depot was part of the '1883 Agreement' to provide goods handling and warehousing facilities for Tilbury Docks. The site was the LTS Whitechapel Goods Branch, between Fenchurch Street and Stepney, with the Depot incorporating a warehouse (above) for the Dock Company's use. The contract was let to Mowlem and work commenced in late 1884 after some details had been altered, requiring a reapplication to Parliament. The Goods Depot was ready for use for dock traffic when Tilbury Dock opened on 17 April 1886 but the warehouses were not handed over to the Dock Company

Ahoy there. The left-hand end of the landing stage is for liners; a Gravesend ferry is berthed middle of picture. The large vessel on the extreme left is in the Tidal Basin.

until August 1887. The LTS already had running powers to Commercial Road by an 1876 Agreement which had granted them for goods trains as far as Goodman's Yard a little further west. Commercial Road Depot also dealt with general LTS goods traffic from 1 July 1886. There were four floors above the shed which formed the warehouse, principally used to store tea. It had a capacity of 171,000 chests and a small part was set aside for bonded silk. Six shipping lines had a presence there.

6. SHIPPING

Gravesend has a history of water transport and a million passengers a year had made a journey on the London service as early as 1815. With the railway coming to Tilbury in 1854 ferry services began from there to Gravesend Town Pier and to Rosherville in the hope of tapping the new traffic. Until 1880 the LTS ferry could only carry rail passengers but in that year the company leased the War Department ferry from Tilbury to Gravesend. At the same time it purchased a rival ferry from Gravesend to Tilbury, giving the LTS its own pier at Gravesend West Street; the ferries started using this instead of the Town Pier which was purchased in turn in 1885, when the ferries returned there.

The Gravesend Railway, nominally independent but actually vested in the London, Chatham & Dover, opened its line from Fawkham Junction, between Swanley and Rochester, to Gravesend West Street on 1 May 1886. The 'ceremonial' opening had been on 17 April, the same day as the opening of Tilbury Docks. Indeed, part of the general junketing included a tug trip to inspect the new Docks.

Boat trains also ran to Gravesend Pier (at West Street) to service 'Batavia Line' sailings to Rotterdam between 1916 and 1939. After the Second World War these transferred to Tilbury and Gravesend West closed to passengers on 3 August 1953, with freight following in 1968.

Little is on record concerning the LTS shipping fleet but it is known that the Company's fleet in 1895 consisted of five steamers including the paddle steamer 'Tilbury' built in 1883. Details of a further five vessels have come to light, all constructed by A.W. Robertson of London:

S.S. Carlotta 1893, 261 gross tons, withdrawn 1930.

S.S. Gertrude 1906, 255 gross tons, sold 1932.

S.S. Edith 1911, 283 gross tons, withdrawn 1961.

S.S. Rose 1901, 259 gross tons, withdrawn 1961.

S.S. Catherine 1903, 259 gross tons.

'Catherine' could convey 648 passengers, 'Rose' 655 and 'Edith' 650. As well as serving as ferries the steamers were used as tenders taking passengers to and from the liners lying off Tilbury. They came under the supervision of the grandly titled 'Locomotive, Carriage and Wagon and Marine Superintendent', one Mr Whitelegg. 'Gertrude' passed to the Medway Steam Packet Co and was renamed 'Rochester Queen'. She was resold in 1933 and again renamed. She was not broken up (as a tender) until 1962.

In April 1954 125 staff were involved in the shipping side of the business at Tilbury and Gravesend, operating five twin screw vessels. At this time, nearly four million passengers per annum were being conveyed, plus a quarter of a million bicycles. The vehicle ferry ceased operation in 1961 when the Dartford road tunnel opened. Following the transfer of the passenger ferry, from West Street to the Town Pier at Gravesend in 1885, West Street still dealt with the goods and cattle. Through bookings to Gravesend remained available from all LTS stations. Town Pier finally closed to passengers in 1965, after which vessels used West Street Landing Stage.

7. SIGNALLING

The earliest boxes recorded are those at Tilbury East and West Junctions; little more than huts on

Royal Mail Lines RMS HIGHLAND PRINCESS, built in 1930, 17 March 1956. Photograph Philip J. Kelley.

elevated platforms they appeared in 1854. Both were extended for interlocking in 1876. It was as late as 1906 before the East Junction box was replaced. Tilbury South Junction was 'different' in that it had two frames of 72 levers opposite one another, totalling 144 – though a Board of Trade Report of 1928 refers to 140 levers. It dated from 29 July 1906 and closed in 1961 when a modern BR box at Riverside took over. This lasted until 5 April 1996 when all was centralised at Upminster.

6. TILBURY ENGINE SHED

The original shed was of timber

The less-than welcoming shell of Tilbury shed in 1954, 42252 amid the desolation. With the economy getting going again the labour shortages that were to plague the LTS Section right through to electrification were already being felt – witness the clinker all around the shed. Photograph H.C. Casserley.

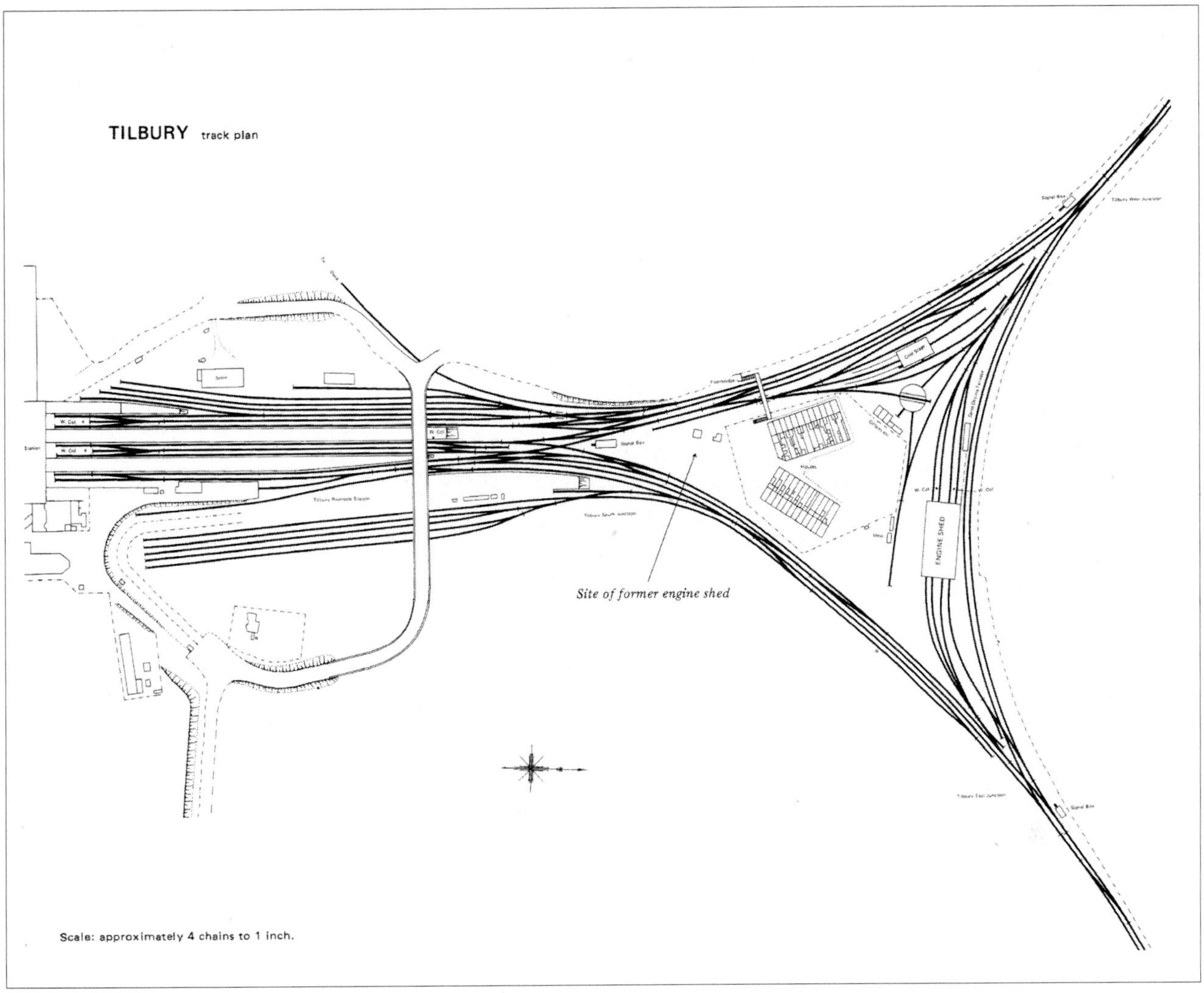

TILBURY track plan

ENGINE SHED

Site of former engine shed

Scale: approximately 4 chains to 1 inch.

Tilbury shed, with the clouds lending an unexpected drama to a very unprepossessing building, 20 March 1956. This is the 'new' shed; that is, with a fresh cladding of corrugated iron. Following particularly vitriolic complaints of time keeping in the early 1950s the young Allan Garraway was despatched to record some of the dismal conditions under which locomotives were made ready. At Tilbury the sides and roof were rusted and holed but the wooden smoke chutes were literally falling in (dangerous) pieces. When BR refurbished the shed it didn't bother with new smoke chutes, just widened the doorways and hoped the wind would do the rest.

More luxury at Tilbury; a wonderful assortment of bothies on 14 September 1957 included, prominently, a Midland Pullman car, the pre-diesel one that is! Photograph H.C. Casserley.

construction and most likely dated from the opening of the line in 1854 or very soon after. It had two shed roads and two short sidings, for the coal wagons and the engine being coaled. It was replaced in 1906 by a four road corrugated iron structure designed to house sixteen of the 4-4-2Ts Coded 13C in the LMS 1935 scheme, Tilbury passed to the Eastern Region on 20 February 1949 and subsequently became 33B. Refurbishment came only late in its life and it was 1956 in fact before the rusting shell was renewed – again in corrugated iron! It lost its allocation with electrification in June 1962 but survived another three months as a 'servicing point'.

7. LOCOMOTIVES

Mainstay of work at Tilbury for many years were inevitably the LTS 4-4-2Ts. As the years progressed several 0-6-0 tender engines arrived, firstly in the shape of MR No.3035 and later the only two genuine LTS tender locos, LMS Nos.2898 and 2699 built in 1898 for the Ottoman Railway in Turkey. They were built by Sharp Stewart but cancelled by the purchasers after being built. The 'Tilbury' then took them on.

The 3 cylinder Stanier tanks built for the LTS Section, though daily visitors were not normally allocated at Tilbury but inevitably one slipped the net and 2522 was there in November 1945. 2500 itself was exhibited at Riverside when new, together with the latest first class corridor coach. At Nationalisation, Tilbury boasted eighteen 4-4-2Ts, an 0-6-2T, four Fairburn 2-6-4Ts which had arrived in June 1946 and two 0-6-0s, a 2F and a 4F. The latter worked as Grays pilots. If not available, an 0-6-2T did the honours.

In January 1954 Standard tanks 80069-80073 inclusive arrived, ousting 4-4-2Ts 41936, 41949, 41950, 41969 and 41970, leaving only 41945 and 41946 of the class to see that year out at Tilbury. In May 1954 80080 arrived to see off Fairburn 42221 and 80079 followed to push 42222 out. This left just five Fairburns, 42218, 42219, 42220, 42223 and 42224 which were replaced by Standards 80074-80078 at the end of 1956. At this time,

One of the three railwaymen's terraces which once stood inside the triangle, March 1953. The north one (this is 'East Row', one of two shown on the shed plan) was demolished some years after the new shed was built. That's the east end of the shed beyond – this truly was 'living on top of the job'. Photograph H.C. Casserley.

LTS 0-6-2T 41984 on the turntable road, 15 March 1952. The disastrous East Coast floods the following year, of January-February 1953, completely disrupted workings at Tilbury. The shed was inundated leaving a number of locomotives marooned – 4-4-2Ts, some 0-6-2Ts and one or two 2-6-4Ts. One result was some unexpected 'casual' jobs for Bow Works; salt flood water had got into axleboxes and as soon as the affected engines could be moved they were taken gingerly away to Bow. Only a couple of hot bearings resulted, surprisingly, and replacement engines equipped with the Hudd ATC (itself severely affected by the flood water) were rustled up from Kentish Town and Cricklewood. Photograph Philip J. Kelley.

having almost approached 'standardisation', more strange locomotives appeared than ever before. With the closure of Upminster sub-shed in September 1956, more work passed to Tilbury and N7 0-6-2Ts, push and pull fitted, arrived in the shape of 69691, 69694, 69695 and 69698 as well as (even more startling, this) an ex-GN C12 4-4-2T, 67363. 69691 was replaced by 69679 in November 1957. These lasted until dieselisation of the Upminster-Grays service on 6 January 1958. The N7s saw off the last of the Tilbury 4-4-2Ts and indeed the Midland 0-4-4Ts of which only one, 58091, was latterly at Tilbury.

By now, electrification work was imminent and WD 2-8-0s, in the shape of 90106 and 90494 arrived in March 1958 followed by 90034 and 90093 later in the year. These were mainly used on the electrification works trains, 90093 being so involved at Ockendon in November 1958 and 90034 at Tilbury on a structure cementing train in July 1959. When Plaistow shed lost its allocation (it became a 'sub' of Tilbury!) on 2 November 1959, Tilbury acquired (on paper at least) six more WDs, three 0-6-0 3F 'jinty' tanks plus half a dozen J39s. The 0-6-0s were condemned in March 1960.

When the end finally came in the summer of 1962, the Standard 2-6-4Ts went to Stratford, to March and to both ends of the Central Wales line. The Fairburns were mostly condemned and the WDs went into store. Apart from electrification of the passenger service, diesels from Ripple Lane were covering most of the freight work.

No mention of locomotive working at Tilbury would be complete without mention of the boat trains and the variety of visiting locos on other passenger and freight work. The Boat Specials from St Pancras, initially worked by Midland 2P 4-4-0s, later became regular 4F and Crab 2-6-0 jobs. As time progressed Ivatt 4MTs in the 43000 series appeared, then the Class 5s and indeed Standard Class 5s in their turn. The problem arose if workings were not 'balanced'. Such an occasion was 18 April 1952 which saw J17 0-6-0 65545 working a Boat Special to St Pancras.

Special traffic of the 'irregular' kind brought SR light Pacifics (34104 turned on Tilbury triangle on 8 July 1957 after working a special to Ockendon) and B1, B2 and B17 4-6-0s off the GE Section. J17s, J19 and J20 0-6-0s, K3 2-6-0s, LM 8Fs and Black 5s were regular visitors, and even ex-GW 28XX 2-8-0s at one time. The story of the one that was wrongly allocated to a job at Tilbury and finished up at Harlow Mill is well known. Regular turns included both ER 9F 2-10-0s on Fisons services from Immingham to Thames Haven and for a while, a Feltham Q1 which worked in with tanks from Micheldever to Thames Haven and took its 'layover' on Tilbury shed before returning. 33018 was the loco on 18 July 1959.

Finally, even North British diesel 10800 (see for instance *Diesel Dawn* in BRILL Vol.11 No.8, May 2002) worked into the area between 29 December 1954 and 21 January 1955, while 'on loan' to Plaistow 'in connection with the possible working of goods trains and excursion traffic from outside sections when the proposed electrification of the LTS line is completed' – it was 7½ years later.

With acknowledgements to Peter Kay's two volume History of the LT&S, to the Great Eastern Society and to the Public Record Office at Kew.

One of the endless Boat Specials, M806 arriving at Tilbury Riverside behind Cricklewood's Ivatt 2-6-0 43118 on 20 March 1954. This service was running in connection with the sailing of P&O's liner CHUSAN to the Far East. Photograph Philip J. Kelley.

LTS 4-4-2T 55 BOW ROAD built in 1900 and first named WELLINGTON ROAD, ready to leave Riverside with a full train of four wheeled stock for Fenchurch Street soon after the 1906 station reconstruction. From the onlookers and the condition of the locomotive, it may have been a special occasion. The loco, which was renamed in 1903, became 2162 in 1912 and 2096 in 1929. It was one of those which wandered northwards in later years and was retired from Nottingham in June 1950. At such places, away from crews familiar with them, they were unpopular and unloved.

The station from Ferry Road bridge on 20 March 1956. The carriage cleaners and maintenance staff are dealing with 'off peak' stabled non-corridor stock. The length of the platforms is particularly apparent here. The River and Kent are beyond.

On 20 March 1956, one of the type built for the line, a Stanier 3-cylinder 2-6-4T, waits with non-corridor stock and an ex-LNER gangwayed luggage van. Note the ground signal at the foot of the right-hand platform starter.

Looking north through Ferry Road bridge where a 4-4-2T sits as Carriage Pilot. The bridge was constructed so that Ferry Road could be diverted as part of the 1920s station reconstruction. It crossed eighteen running lines and sidings.

This is Tilbury South Junction with lines diverging left to Grays and right to Pitsea. This box (established 1906) contained two 72 lever frames. It lasted until 1961 when a new Tilbury Riverside box took over. The two remaining rows of railway cottages can be seen either side of the box. Note the unusual Midland signal with both a route indicator and a distant signal banner on the same post.

The footbridge from Ferry Road to the railway cottages, showing more Midland signalling and the loco coal stage. The line between the engine shed and the cottages leads to the turntable. The latter was a bit of a luxury most of the time with a triangle handy and the majority of the complement tank engines. Note the 'London Transport' bus stop sign on the left. Yes, Country Area did reach Tilbury Ferry in those days, with a through route from Romford.

Tilbury Town North Junction with its First World War Midland style Box. We are looking from the west end of the Exchange Sidings towards Grays.

REPTON AT THE ROYAL RACES

An inevitably immaculate 30926 REPTON heads a Royal train for the Derby at Epsom, from Victoria to Tattenham Corner past Clapham Junction on 31 May 1961. The train was made up of Pullman cars ISLE OF THANET, ARIES and NIOBE with ex-LNER Royal Saloon No.396; a fortnight before the same vehicles had carried the Royal party (behind 34009 LYME REGIS) to the consecration of Guildford Cathedral. Photograph John Scrace.

REPTON again, a day or two later at Clapham Junction, with the same train but this time bound for the Oaks at Epsom; Victoria-Tattenham Corner, 2 June 1961. Photograph John Scrace.

REPTON ready for Royal duty again, at Stewarts Lane shed a year later on 6 June 1962. The wiring rigged up at the rear of the tender is worthy of note; in later years with advancing technology a telephone line was set up between the train and the Inspector who always rode in the cab on such Royal occasions. The Southern was forever involved in these important state trains, having taken the President of the Ivory Coast up from Southampton Docks to Victoria only two days before for his visit to Britain. On that day there had, incredibly, been four standby engines; in addition to 34089 602 SQUADRON on the President's special there was 34045 OTTERY ST. MARY at Southampton Docks, 34104 BERE ALSTON at Eastleigh, 34071 601 SQUADRON at Basingstoke and 34017 ILFRACOMBE at Woking. Photographs John Scrace.

After its careful preparation, REPTON takes its leave of Stewarts Lane on the rear of the Royal stock on its way empty (except for various officers, attendants and so on) to form the Victoria-Tattenham Corner train. On that Derby Day, 6 June 1962, there were no less than three standby engines, another Schools 30901 WINCHESTER and, surprisingly, two K Moguls, 32343 and 32353. Photograph John Scrace.

It is now 8 June 1962, and this time REPTON hurries the Royal coaches to the Oaks, through Clapham Junction. You can see the shine on the buffers from this far off. Photograph John Scrace.

The top of Camden bank in August 1959. Jubilee 45631 TANGANYIKA forges north with an express, passing 46236 CITY OF BRADFORD which has come down light from Euston, on its way to Camden shed. Photograph Prorail UK (Durrant)/The Transport Treasury.

BIG 'UNS, NORTH AND SOUTH

A breathtaking show of Pacific power at the south end of Carlisle Citadel in the early 1960s. Left to right are 46234 DUCHESS OF ABERCORN, 46211 QUEEN MAUD and 46227 DUCHESS OF DEVONSHIRE. Photograph Geoff Goslin Collection.

TRAIN No.1

As American railroads go, the Norfolk and Western Railway, as it termed itself, was not in the top flight for size, operating in 1955 2,128 route miles with 428 steam and eight diesel locomotives. Its purpose in life was to transport coal from the coalfield of West Virginia (extending from Bluefield through Williamson to Prichard, about 160 miles in extent) down to Lamberts Point, near Norfolk, bordering on Chesapeake Bay and the Atlantic Ocean. From Williamson to Norfolk was over 450 miles so it was by no means a South Wales valley operation clanking down grade to Barry Docks or wherever for about 30 miles or so for there were four distinct summits to tackle en route. The main line was Norfolk-Cincinnati with branches to Columbus, Bristol, Winston-Salem, Durham and Hagerstown (see map). Columbus to Norfolk was mainly double-tracked but elsewhere single was the rule. Roanoke was the pivot of the system and where the headquarters and locomotive shops were located. Passenger services were subsidised by the coal traffic which was the staple; in 1955 nearly 52 million (short) tons of bituminous coal were handled.

Apart from a litany of English sounding names (Crewe, Poole, Bedford and Windsor among them) and the re-gauging of the line from Norfolk to Bristol on 1 June 1886 – all 408 miles were converted in one day to standard gauge – there was little or no affinity with anything British. A great attraction in the mid-1950s was that it still was a steam line, the policy being to use the product of the coalfield which it served, rather than rely on oil fuel. To this end the installations were equipped with 'throughput' shed facilities of a high order and, to save time taking water en route, a second tender was attached to many of the freight locomotives. However, in the Fall of 1956 it was known that this steam bastion had been breached. The walls had not collapsed Jericho-fashion but rather had been undermined for the diesels had been ordered in quantity. Rumour was rife that (a)

Norfolk & Western Railway westbound freight passing through Roanoke in charge of 2-8-8-2 class Y6 No.2171 fitted with auxiliary tender.

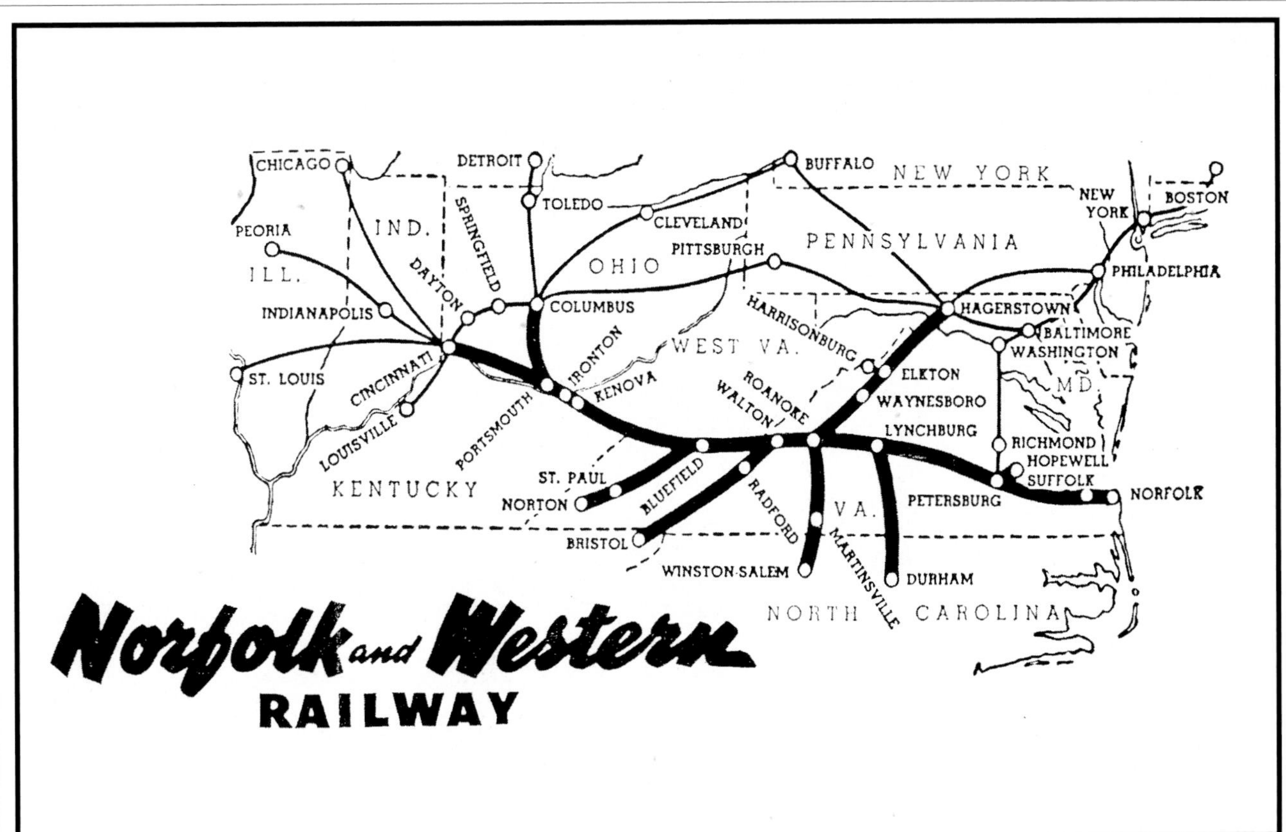

CHICAGO
DETROIT
TOLEDO
BUFFALO
NEW YORK
BOSTON
PEORIA
IND.
ILL.
SPRINGFIELD
DAYTON
CLEVELAND
OHIO
PITTSBURGH
PENNSYLVANIA
PHILADELPHIA
INDIANAPOLIS
COLUMBUS
HARRISONBURG
HAGERSTOWN
BALTIMORE
WASHINGTON
MD.
ST. LOUIS
CINCINNATI
LOUISVILLE
IRONTON
KENOVA
PORTSMOUTH
WEST VA.
ELKTON
WAYNESBORO
ROANOKE
WALTON
LYNCHBURG
RICHMOND
HOPEWELL
SUFFOLK
NORFOLK
PETERSBURG
KENTUCKY
ST. PAUL
NORTON
BLUEFIELD
RADFORD
VA.
BRISTOL
WINSTON-SALEM
MARTINSVILLE
DURHAM
NORTH CAROLINA
Norfolk and Western
RAILWAY

Sunshine and shadow in Shaffers Crossing (Roanoke) shed. Nos.379 and 2122 nearest camera, 10 November 1956.

these machines were working already or (b) they were arriving next month or (c) the month after that.

To an Englishman working temporarily in New York this was a challenge difficult to let pass. Elsewhere in the United States of America there were still pockets of steam to be sniffed out but nothing on the scale of the Norfolk & Western and so negotiations for passes to visit Roanoke shops and locomotive depot were completed and one Friday evening our traveller toddled off to the Pennsylvania station in New York to join the 6.10pm Pennsylvania Railroad train to Harrisburg which included a N&W sleeping car running through to Roanoke. Such luxury, however, could not be indulged in because

10 November 1956, and Norfolk & Western J class 4-8-4 No.611 pulls out of Roanoke southbound with THE TENNESSEAN.

Shaffers Crossing 10 November 1956, with shed switcher W6 class 0-8-0T No.821 on the vast turntable – observe that drop into the pit!

the currency regulations had to be observed to some degree (at this time, because of the parlous state of the UK's finances, only business trips which drew in dollars to the homeland were allowed) and so at Harrisburg a change had to be made to a N&W coach which was provided through to Roanoke via Hagerstown. PRR train No.31 THE SPIRIT OF ST LOUIS (the 6.10pm) was powered by one of the classic GG1 class electric locomotives but at Harrisburg train No.645 was diesel hauled and this machine quickly demonstrated its inadequacy so that by the time Hagerstown was reached at some time after 1am, late and cold through lack of heating, any enjoyment of US railroading had evaporated.

At Hagerstown the sleeping car, the coach and two baggage cars became Norfolk & Western's train No.1, so hopes arose. The next 238 miles to Roanoke, it was expected, would be behind steam power and so it was. The 106 miles to Shenandoah included nine stops out of the 18 stations shown in the timetable, including a 25-minute halt at Shenandoah Junction. A daily (except Sundays) mixed train served all 18 stations in each direction but beyond Shenandoah there was no service on offer other than by train No.1 and its counterpart No.2 in the other direction. From Shenandoah to Roanoke the 132½ miles was scheduled to take 4 hours and 5 minutes with 21 intermediate stops. The make-up (or consist) of the train was increased by the attachment of a diner at Shenandoah but, even so, a 5-car train was not much of a load for the K2s class streamlined 4-8-2 No.128. So far as the engine was concerned it was a case of 'mutton done-up lamb' because No.128 had been built way back in 1923 having had the streamlining and maybe other modernisations added in mid-life. Warmth and then daylight both contributed to the revivification of the traveller who, after noting by experience that the lavatory basin in the toilet of the coach lacked an anti-splash rim, repaired to the diner for a welcome breakfast to complete the raising of spirits and expectations.

The first sighting of a class Y6b 2-8-8-2 on a freight was at Buena Vista – an appropriately named place! – and more followed over the last 50 miles to Roanoke where, on the approach to the station, a Y3a class 2-8-8-2 was caught sight of outside the works. On arrival a guide presented himself for a conducted tour of the workshops. No! the diesels hadn't arrived so far but it was a fairly close-run thing. The works did seem to be preparing for the event for, apart from the works shunting engine (W6 class 0-8-0 tank No.800 dating from 1898) there were just three engines in for shopping, Nos.1231 (2-6-6-4 A class), 2161 (2-8-8-2 Y6a) and 2195 (2-8-8-2 Y6b). The guide explained that one of the factors contributing to the change in motive power was the inability to obtain replacement fittings for steam engines from outside sources because most firms had abandoned catering for steam traction. In 1955, the previous year, no less than 296 locomotives had been repaired in these shops.

A limousine was provided as transport to the locomotive depot which was situated a mile or so west of the station at a point known as Shaffers Crossing. The depot design was on the basis of straight-line servicing proceeding on the same track throughout – a sort of conveyor belt with the engine moving itself from inspection, ash disposal, lubrication, sand, water and coal replenishment, high pressure cleaning and turning. Shaffers Crossing, though the largest depot, was not an isolated example of advanced thinking on servicing locomotives for each of the depots at Bluefield, Williamson, Portsmouth, Winston-Salem and Petersburg had its own covered 'lubritorium' (what a splendidly concocted American word!) and high towers for delivering sand and coal. The K2 4-8-2 off the arrival at Roanoke station at 1.15pm, for example, will have run to the depot and have finished the complete service by 2.50pm, 1½ hours being standard for most classes. Up to 140 engines have been dealt with

Twilight of steam on the Norfolk & Western, 10 November 1956, with J class No.612 standing at Roanoke on the northbound THE TENNESSEAN. Shenandoah Valley line to left and locomotive shops right background.

in a 24-hour period at Shaffers Crossing. For those with a liking for figures (1955 vintage) Shaffers Crossing depot employed 894 persons, serviced 27,824 engines – or 76 per day – during the year and softened 4,187,000 gallons of water per day. It had a single 40-stall roundhouse and two locomotive servicing buildings and maintained the motive power for five locomotive districts.

A total of 42 engines was noted during the visit, a lot passing through for service, some under repair and some seemingly withdrawn especially, in this last category, some M class 4-8-0s. The shed switcher was No.821, similar to that at the works and was the oldest locomotive present having been built in 1899; then, in longevity, came Nos.379, 405, 496 all 4-8-0s of 1906. There was one S1a 0-8-0, No.232 of 1953, the youngest of all, other than No.2300 which will be mentioned shortly, a couple of simple 2-6-6-4s of class A (Nos.1220 and 1223 of 1936), 2-8-8-2s of various Y class sub-divisions and Z1b classification, three J 4-8-4 streamliners and some 4-8-2 streamliners too.

Most interesting of the lot was No.2300 a coal fired, steam turbine electric drive engine of 6-6-6-6 wheel arrangement, all wheels driving. This machine, built in May 1954 (Baldwin works No.75911) was by way of experiment to see if coal could be harnessed to provide energy for generators to power axle-mounted traction motors. Just over 160 feet long with tender attached, No.2300 looked like a diesel with 6-wheeled (3 feet 6ins in diameter) power bogies under it. There was storage space for 20 tons of coal and the tender held 22,000 gallons of water. A 600lb/sq.in pressure watertube boiler produced steam at 900 degrees Fahrenheit which fed into a turbine with a 4,500 horsepower output which was translated into direct current in the generators to work the 21 axle-mounted traction motors geared for a top speed of 60mph. All of this appeared to be a complicated way to challenge diesel power. So had the experiment been concluded-successful-unsuccessful-aborted? The non-committal answer provided was that No.2300 was awaiting replacement parts. Maybe, but one wondered, with the smell of diesels on the wind, if the future held anything for it.

A shed visit can last for only so long, even with the sophisticated operation to be seen at Shaffers Crossing, so it was time to witness the traffic, mainly mineral, rolling through Roanoke. To obtain a photograph of 100 gondolas behind an articulated locomotive usually with auxiliary tender was, of course, impossible; if a picture of engine and second tender could be worked into the frame it was good going! After this the Roanoke shed of the Virginian Railway was visited although not by arrangement; here there were electric, steam and diesel traction all in the same shed. There was a 3-unit electric and three diesel-electrics present and 14 steam engines all of which were dead except for four 0-8-0s. Of the ten not in steam there were a couple of BA class 2-8-4s, an AG class 2-6-6-6, three 2-8-2s (MCA class) and four Pacifics of the PA class, one of which, No.212, had worked the final (steam or otherwise) passenger service from Norfolk to Roanoke on the previous 29 January. The Virginian Railway ran a parallel southerly service to the Norfolk & Western between these points.

For the 6.30pm return journey from Roanoke on train No.2 it was No.128 again with the same sort of consist, if not the very same, as had

Norfolk & Western Railway Train No.1 halts at Troutville, headed by K2a class 4-8-2 No.128, November 1956.

Pennsylvania Railroad class M1 4-8-2 No.6738 on 11 November 1956, getting to grips with a westbound freight shortly after leaving Enola Yards, near Harrisburg.

Reading Railroad class T1 4-8-4 No.2115 travelling with caboose near Enola while on loan to Pennsylvania Railroad, 11 November 1956.

come down on No.1 that morning. Full advantage was taken of the diner before it was hooked off at Shenandoah. Of alighting at Harrisburg at 3.40am, if it was that time (perhaps the diesel had lost time again from Hagerstown) little may be remarked except that it is peculiar what drives the enthusiast's desire to see steam locomotives at work. Here the attraction was an upsurge in freight traffic which had found the Pennsylvania short of power causing Reading Railroad 4-8-4s to be called in to assist. Observation out at Enola confirmed the impression of massiveness that the American trains gave as box cars, gondolas and cabooses hurtled along behind steam with the tracks completely unfenced; they could – indeed did at times – come to grief when the axle-boxes ran hot and seized up and the wagons strew themselves all over the railroad in disarray if nothing worse. Lineside observers would not stand much chance to get out of the way!

And so to train No.32 THE ST LOUISAN, the 1.18pm from Harrisburg, with electric GG1 No.4937 at the head end to New York after a never-to-be-repeated weekend (of almost) unalloyed bliss!

Not a Richard Branson offshoot but Virginian Railroad class PA 4-6-2 No.215 out of use at Roanoke shed after withdrawal of passenger services, 10 November 1956.

Three of the late and much missed Dr Ian C. Allen's magnificent photographs from the 1930s. His work is probably best remembered for all those marvellously evocative and highly technically adept images across East Anglia in the 1950s. Before the War (in which he served in the Medical Corps) he roved further afield and while some of the efforts were less than wholly successful essays in the craft, the best was startlingly good. These three show, firstly, Duke 4-4-0 3259 MERLIN at Portmadoc in June 1937. By that year this little engine, costing £1,990 2d with its original 2,000 gallon tender back in 1895, had run up some 1,150,000 miles. The 0-6-0ST 2194 KIDWELLY is on the Weymouth Quay line some time in the 1930s (it arrived in March 1926 and left in August 1941) while Star 4-6-0 4007 SWALLOWFIELD PARK is at Kingham, in June 1937. It was not finally withdrawn until 1951. All photographs Dr Ian C. Allen, The Transport Treasury.

Lure of the Big Top

Three fine views from above – unusual and always welcome. We have no details of time or place unfortunately but one or two things can be inferred or guessed at. Those canopies and their massive concrete supports behind Caprotti Black 5 44750, for years a Longsight engine, are suggestive of Derby station for instance. The location of V2 60875 and A3 60100 SPEARMINT is equally obscure. Both are obviously late in day, from their lousy condition. The Pacific bears a 64A St Margarets shedplate; always a Scottish engine, she went there from Haymarket in January 1963 and was withdrawn in June 1965, so that leaves us with 'almost certainly Scotland, about 1964'. The V2 must be at the very end of its life. A Doncaster engine from 1959 to withdrawal, yet again it could be anywhere, yet strangely, Peterborough seems to suggest itself. It was condemned in March 1962 and cut up at Doncaster Works; it already has its electrification flashes so this sombre event could hardly have been many months off when this picture was taken. All photographs The Transport Treasury

60100

View From A Bridge

Above. And another 'Spot The Join' composite from the cutting edge laboratories of Irwell Press. This is the fabulous London vista (when the only tall structures were chimneys or gasometers) at Willesden, 11 April 1964. As ever these clever technical efforts must involve a compromise and eagle-eyed readers will instantly spot the somewhat staggered single line in the foreground. It was either this, or distort the noble London skyline into a peculiar mound, creating a substantial hill where none exists. As it is, it does trail away somewhat unnaturally to the right, to the south. Still this is the price we pay for the chance to view such places as 'an environment' and what a lovely view it is, from the new Power Box on the other side of the main lines (extreme left), to the vast monolith of the coaling plant, the strange cone-like roof of the roundhouse beyond the shed just to the left of the high water tank and, finally, to the Grand Union canal at the extreme right. Note the sidewalls still projecting out into the shed yard and its ranks of engines; these are the mortal remains of the extension, completed on Webb's orders in 1898. The original portion behind dated from the 1870s. It was the later part, however, that did not stand the test of time and it was removed in the 1930s. The photographer was unlucky to catch Willesden without a single Coronation Pacific on view (up to seven could be seen at one time that summer) though one or two may be lurking out of sight. Still, there are at least four Jubilees among the serried ranks. The photographer is standing on the bridge parapet of the 'Acton Branch', the old Midland line which ran south from Cricklewood Yard (diving under the Edgware Road) to make an important freight link at Acton Wells Junction with the North and South Western Junction line. It was along this line, no doubt, that the two Southern Region engines had come, via Feltham, maybe, on their way north (Kettering perhaps?) for scrap. Made up into a train with brake and two opens in between, U1 31894 and K Moguls 32343 (both once of Brighton – see the first article by Bryan Wilson at the front of this Annual) have been set back into the siding holding the crane and an out of use Jinty tank. To return to the somewhat staggered single line in the foreground; this had originally continued across the canal but the bridge was removed and for years it served simply as a siding. BR reinstated it using the original abutments and it formed a useful through route from the West Coast main line to Acton Wells Junction – it was even used on occasion for diverted passenger trains.

Left, a 'ground level' view of the K Mogul in the yard a little later, when a BR Class 5 has hoved into view. Someone in an unfeasibly white shirt has boarded 32343... Photographs R.C. Riley.

Fifties Freight Around Buxton

At the centre of activity, the junction at Buxton No.1, Buxton's 48462 heads south onto the Ashbourne line in August 1952 watched by the bobby in the door of the box. The lines beyond the shadow of the engine are those of the Buxton Curve whilst in the background, stark against the upland scenery, are the old and new coal stages and other buildings of the Motive Power Depot. The lines coming in from the left emanate from the Nor'West station. These are surmounted by the tracks of the Down Sidings and it can be readily understood why they were, as often as not, referred to as the 'Top Sidings'. Photograph: E.R. Morten.

High on the southern tip of the Pennine Chain, in the area known as the White Peak and well above the 1,000 feet contour, sits the Derbyshire spa town of Buxton, *Aquae Arnemetiae*, 'assumed to be the highest market town in England' according to Arthur Mee in his 'The King's England: Derbyshire' (Hodder & Stoughton 1937). The first steam railway in the vicinity was the Cromford & High Peak Railway, completed in 1831, which traversed the moors a mile and a half or so south of the town at Harpur Hill. Next to arrive, in June 1863, was the Midland Railway's Rowsley & Buxton line followed almost immediately by the LNWR's Stockport, Disley & Whaley Bridge line. These terminated in twin passenger train sheds but between the Midland's Buxton East Junction and the LNWR's Buxton No.1 signal boxes a steeply rising connection, known as the Buxton Curve, allowed freight traffic transfer between the adjacent railways. Relationships between the two companies was somewhat frigid, however, so the Midland pressed ahead with its own drive to the north-west in the form of the Rowsley & Buxton Extension line, opened in 1866. This crossed the mountainous divide at Peak Forest then burrowed under the LNWR near Dove Holes in the notorious 2,984 yard tunnel of the same name. Finally, following an Act of 1890, the LNWR, which had by then assimilated the Cromford & High Peak, was enabled to abandon the latter's route north of Ladmanlow, lay a new double track line from

By Keith Miles

Buxton to Parsley Hay having junctions with the original C&HP tracks both there and at Hindlow, and extend a thirteen mile single track branch southwards to Ashbourne. All this was in place by late summer 1899 and completed the railway map of the area.

The bleak uplands around Buxton were (and remain) the source of an exceptionally pure limestone and small scale quarrying and lime-burning had been carried on for centuries. With the coming of improved transport, especially the railways, the quarrying business boomed such that by the period under review the bulk of the traffic was mineral. Best known, perhaps were 'The Tunstead Hoppers', eight daily 8F hauled trains each comprising sixteen 40 ton vacuum-braked bogie hopper wagons of 1930s vintage giving a total load behind the tender of well in excess of 1,000 tons. Between them, the adjacent Tunstead and Park Forest establishments, which presented a near four mile continuous quarry face to the railway, yielded over seven million tons annually. To this must be added the outputs from other locations in the area such as Millers Dale, Topley Pike, Ashwood Dale, Hindlow and the Cromford & High Peak sites. All this was, of course, only locally produced traffic but from further afield, toiling up the bank from Rowsley, came around thirty coal trains each weekday from Nottinghamshire and North Derbyshire plus a couple of iron ore from Northamptonshire. Further to this considerable volume of mineral traffic was the necessary reciprocal flow of empty wagons plus the normal carriage of goods and merchandise.

An impression of the railway map in the Buxton area showing all the salient features – elevations, gradients, stations, signal boxes, loops and sidings although the latter are, of necessity, somewhat simplified.

The Midland 1 in 89 approach to Buxton as it climbs across Fairfield Road bridge to East Junction. Spanning the tracks into the Midland Station is the Ashbourne line on the Buxton Viaduct. One operating feature of the Buxton Curve was that light engines released from the Midland Station were allowed to go 'wrong road' on the up line in order to get to the loco shed without any conflicting movements at No.1 junction. An engine can be discerned doing just that and the small shunt ahead signal to the right of the tracks is still pulled off. Photograph: H. Townley courtesy J.M. Bentley.

May 1951 and the 5.49pm Rowsley-Garston, one of the few mineral trains of the day running under a class H headcode, snakes across Buxton East Junction headed by Widnes' 48558 with a Rowsley banker puffing industriously in the rear. Actually there was a 10mph speed limit over the junction but it's unlikely that the train would achieve any higher speed as it hit the 1 in 66 of the Curve; especially, as in this case, of an inter-divisional service stopping at No.1 box for water and/or a change of crew. Photograph: E.R. Morten

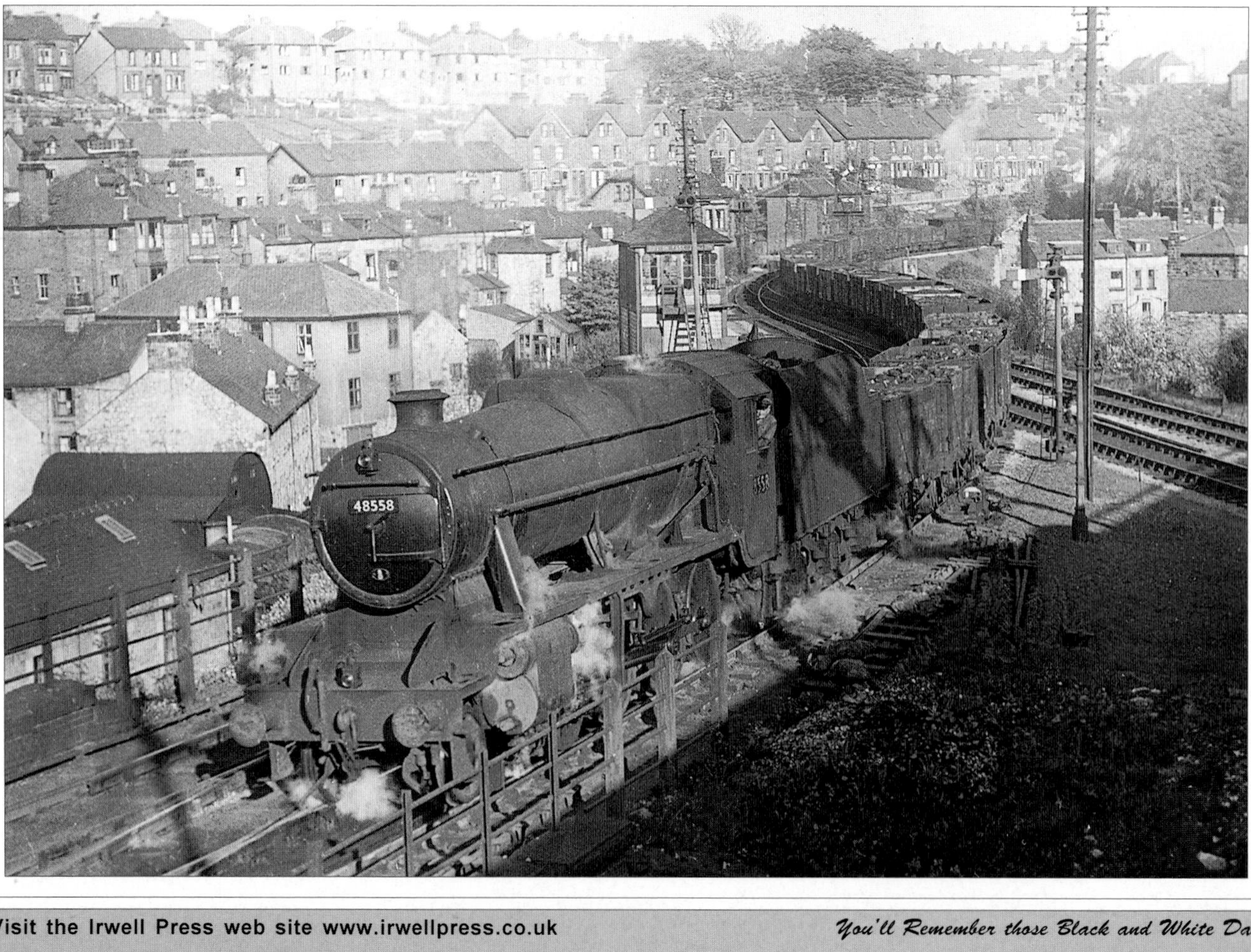

Creeping gingerly out of the Up Sidings onto the Buxton Curve, Rowsley's 44024, one of the shed's 'number fours' with a back cab, heads for home with a class F freight in May 1951. The engine's drifting exhaust partially obscures the four-doll gantry on the Ashbourne line. Incidentally, Rowsley men always referred to the Buxton Curve as 'The Branch'. It was, after all, a branch off their original main line to Buxton. Photograph: E.R. Morten.

In the midst of all this activity sat Buxton MPD providing engines for some of the through services and all of the local requirements. To meet the demands the 1950 allocation included two Crabs, seven Midland 3Fs, three 4Fs, nineteen 8Fs and seven Super Ds: a formidable array of power and one that was needed since a penalty for sitting on top of a hill was the incidence of heavy gradients on the approach lines.

Trains from Rowsley had already endured a fifteen mile climb up the Wye Valley at a ruling gradient of 1 in 90/100 but on passing Buxton East Junction it steepened to a punishing 1 in 66 around the Buxton Curve. After a brief respite past the Up Sidings the 1 in 66 ascent resumed up to the summit at Bibbington's Sidings two miles further on. Following a practice initiated at the turn of the century (see 'Rowsley 17D' in BRILL ANNUAL No.8) trains in excess of 26 loaded mineral wagons or 48 wagons of goods had an assisting engine in the rear, usually provided by Rowsley but Buxton took a share with some of the bankers for trains terminating in their own sidings. Through trains habitually stopped at Buxton No.1 to change footplate crews and/or for the engine to take water and, although the limited length of the Buxton Curve restricted train lengths to 40 wagons, restarting a heavy mineral train, even of this size, on the 1 in 66 gradient was quite a task, especially in adverse weather conditions. One incident where everything didn't go according to plan is recorded in 'Spewing Twos', in BRILL September 2001.

For down trains out of their own sidings Buxton supplied all the bankers, called Targets 65 and 66. These two diagrams between them, in addition to being involved in their marshalling, assisted around a dozen trains daily up to Bibbington's (people seldom added 'Sidings') and the Target 66 engine also assisted the early morning Target 72 tripper up to Briggs Sidings when required. The Ashbourne line curved away from Buxton on a viaduct over the approaches to the Midland station, then across a more spectacular viaduct spanning Duke's Drive. After four and a half miles at a ruling gradient of 1 in 60/62 came the windswept Briggs Sidings, for the ICI and Downlow Lime Works, at 1,260 feet above sea level. Buxton also sent two light engines coupled down to Peak Forest every morning as Targets 78 and 79 for any necessary shunting there and at Tunstead and also to bank the hopper trains on their initial start up the 1 in 90 to Peak Forest summit.

A different problem presented itself for services in the reverse direction; being able to stop! Everyone's heard of the case of John Axon's runaway in February 1957 but, of course, that was a unique case of 48188's steam brake pipe fracturing and the cab being so full of steam that the open regulator couldn't be reached to close it. Rowsley's Syd Curzon was certain, incidentally, that John's frantic popping of the whistle as he bore down the goods loop's 1 in 70 towards Dove Holes was to warn the signalman to get out of his box before the train burst through the dead end stop block and hit it. As it was, the bobby turned it out main line with the resultant fatal collision at Chapel-en-le Frith. Coincidentally Rowsley's Billy Hodkin was firing to Chippy Parkes on the 1.24pm Rowsley-Garston on that particular day. As they emerged from 'the little Wessie tunnel', as Billy called it (the LNWR tunnel, No.96, 104 yards) Chippy called out 'Look here over this side!' 'The dust hadn't settled and you could see wagons piled up sky high,' said Billy,

Above. There were three trains daily to and from the Sheffield area and in May 1951 one of them emerges from the Up Sidings to start the descent down to East Junction. Heading the train is Grimesthorpe's 43683 still in its early BR livery. Beyond the engine the clutter of the local allotments at the foot of the embankment contrasts with the backdrop of bare stone-walled slopes. In common parlance the Up Sidings were known as Donneroo, a corruption of Donahue, the company that laid them. Photograph: E.R. Morten.

Top right. Another BRITISH RAILWAYS 3F, this time Buxton's 43278 setting off with one of the C&HP line services. Despite the instruction in Operating Control Organisation, ERO 52457, that 'engines departing from a Motive Power Depot to work trains, trips or perform shunting, must carry Targets numbered as shown in the Local Trip and Shunting Notices' they were seldom carried. It will be noticed, however, that 43683 in another photograph has 83 chalked on its buffer beam. Photograph: E.R. Morten.

Right. The 4.00pm class K from Buxton climbs the 1 in 63 across Buxton Viaduct on 8 June 1951 on its way to Dovefield Sidings, located some 3½ miles east of Uttoxeter. In charge of the service is Buxton's 49348 and its home depot can be seen in the distance above the train. This particular Super D, having a tender cab, was one of those listed in ERO 62011 as being suitable for coupling to the old LMS wood and steel pattern snowplough. 49210 was the other, plus back-cab 4Fs 43842 and 44382 although the Super Ds were first choice being heavier and stronger. Photograph: E.R. Morten.

'couldn't see no engine.' The normal practice in those days with loose-coupled trains on steep inclines was to pin down a number of wagon brakes. *Goods guards must be careful to securely pin down sufficient brakes to enable Drivers to have complete control of their trains when descending the gradients*, said the Sectional Appendix, *one third of the total number of brakes pinned down should be next to the engine and the remainder at the rear of the train.* For down trains approaching Bibbington's Sidings there was a train engine stop board at the home signal and a bank engine stop board 640 yards further back. With most of the train then being on a short level stretch of track, the guard would walk its length dropping and pinning down brakes as he went. Given the right of way, the banker would assist the train on its passage then, not being coupled up, would drop off, cross over and retreat to Buxton. When Bibbington's Sidings box was closed, the banker followed the train down to Dove Holes before reversing. *When run into the loop or brought to a stand at Dove Holes and the Driver is unable to start, the Guard must lift sufficient brakes in the rear*, the Sectional Appendix instructed, *and when the train is moving to re-*

DOWN — MIDLAND - WESTERN DIVISION SERVICES (In accordance with freight WTT commencing 5·6·58)

Buxton No.1 arr.	dep.	Train			
12·5 W	12·30	10/40	SO }	J	Mineral, Rowsley - Oldham, D
		10/45	SX }		
12·40 L	1·29	11/20	SO	J	Mineral, Rowsley - Longsight, D
1·00 W	1·57	11/35	SO	J	Mineral, Rowsley - Edgeley, D
1·9 W	1·28*	11/55	SX	J	Mineral, Rowsley - Longsight, D
1·20 L	2·42	11/55	SO	J	Mineral, Rowsley - Cheadle Vge. Jn., B
1·43		12·25		J	Mineral, Rowsley - Buxton, BX
		3·55	MX }	J	Mineral, Buxton - Arpley, D
		4·20	MO }		
5·0		3·45	MX }	J	Mineral, Rowsley - Buxton, BX
5·5		3·50	MO }		
6·13		4·55	MO	J	Mineral, Rowsley - Buxton, BX
6·27		4·50	MX	H	Gowhole - Buxton
6·55		5·35		J	Mineral, Rowsley - Buxton, BX
7·19		3·25	MX	J	Mineral, Grimesthorpe - Buxton
7·33		6·15		J	Mineral, Rowsley - Buxton, BX
		9·15	MO }	K	Mineral, Buxton - Longsight, B
			MXQ }		
		9·39		J	Mineral, Buxton - Arpley, B
10·3		6·10	MO	J	Mineral, Grimesthorpe - Buxton
10·13	10·45	8·45	SO	J	Mineral, Rowsley - Edgeley, B
10·40	11·00	8·45	SX	J	Mineral, Rowsley - Heaton Norris, B
		11·20		J	Mineral, Buxton - Hooton, B
11·55 W	12/15	10·30		J	Mineral, Rowsley - Longsight, B
12/32		11·55		J	Mineral, Rowsley - Buxton, BX
		2/6		K	Mineral, Buxton - Edgeley, B
2/10 L	2/30	12/55		J	Mineral, Rowsley - Longsight, B
2/45		11·15		J	Grimesthorpe - Buxton
3/30		2/30		J	T64 Mineral, Millers Dale - Buxton
		3/30		K	T70 Freight, Buxton - Edgeley, B
5/10	5/50	3/55		J	Mineral, Rowsley - {SX Edgeley / SO Longsight} D
		6/55	SX	K	Mineral, Buxton - Longsight, B
7/0	{SO 7/45 / SX 8/38}	5/49		H	Rowsley - Garston, B
		7/12	SO }	H	Buxton - Garston, B
		7/45	SX }		
8/10		4/25		J	Mineral, Grimesthorpe - Buxton
		8/45	SO	K	Buxton - Edgeley, B
		9/28		H	Buxton - Bamfurlong, B
9/45 L	9 57	8/35		J	Mineral, Rowsley - Edgeley, B
		10/19	SX	J	Mineral, Buxton - Edgeley, B
10/48		10/15		K	Mineral, Peak Forest - Buxton
11/49 L	12·2	9/55		J	Rowsley - Garston, D

UP

Buxton No.1 arr.	dep.	Train			
1·34	3·0	10 0	SX	F	Empties, Garston - Kirkby
1·56		11 0	SO	J	Empties, Arpley - Buxton
1·59		11 0	SX	J	Mineral, Arpley - Buxton
2·24		12·39	MX	J	Empties, Davenport Jn. - Buxton
		3·15	MX	J	Empties, Buxton - Rowsley
3·53	4·20	12·25	MX	F	Empties, Garston - Kirkby
4·19		2·20		J	Empties, Longsight - Buxton
		5·45	MO	J	Mineral, Buxton - Sheffield
		6·20		J	Mineral, Buxton - Rowsley
6·30		2·10	MX	H	Widnes, Carter House Jn. - Buxton
7·12		3·5	MX	F	Empties, Garston - Buxton
		8·5		J	Mineral, Buxton - Sheffield
8·6		6·25		H	Edgeley - Buxton
9·45		6·35	MOQ	K	Heaton Norris, Jubilee Sdgs. - Buxton
9·58		7·53	MX	H	Longsight - Buxton
11·0		4·40		H	Edge Hill - Buxton
		11·40	MX	H	Buxton - Rowsley
12/5		5·45		J	Mineral, Garston - Buxton (Assisted from Cheadle Village Jn.)
		12/55		H	Buxton - Rowsley
		1/25		J	T64 Mineral Buxton - Millers Dale
		1/50		J	Mineral, Buxton - Sheffield, Queen's Road (Double headed when required)
2/15		7·48		K	T60 Freight, Edgeley - Buxton
2/26		12/10	SX	H	Longsight - Buxton
2/49	3/20	9·30	SX	J	Empties, Dundas - Kirkby
		4/45		J	Mineral, Buxton - Peak Forest South
5/30		3/5	SO	J	Empties, Longsight - Buxton
		6/50		J	Mineral, Buxton - Rowsley
7/10	7/45	3/48	SO	F	Empties, Latchford Old Line - Kirkby
8/26	9/0	5/29	SO }	H	Stockport - Briggs Sidings
8/54	9/10	6/46	SX }		
		9/5	SX	F	Empties, Buxton - Rowsley
9/48		7/40		J	Mineral, Edgeley - Buxton
		9/58	SO }	J	Mineral, Buxton - Gowhole
		11/5	SX }		
11/13		9/0	SO	J	Empties, Longsight - Buxton
11/13	1·20	6/50	SX	F	Empties, Latchford Old Line - Kirkby

Bankers: BX to Buxton
B to Bibbington's Sidings
D to Dove Holes

Q = As required

KM2002

Table showing the daily Midland-Western interdivisional services plus those starting and terminating at Buxton. The WTT indicates the down trains stopping at Buxton No.1 for water (W), to change engines or trainmen (L) or to follow other trains (*). The WTT on which this table was based was the first to reflect the new BR standard classification of passenger and freight trains. Out went the FF1, FF2, Maltese Cross and so on of the LMS and in came the alphabetic codes used in the table. Explanations for the particular ones included are as follows:

F Express freight not fitted with continuous brake
G Light engine, light engines coupled or engine and brake
H Through freight not running under C, D, E or F headcode
J Mineral or empty wagon train
K Freight or mineral train stopping at intermediate stations.

apply them. Some seven miles further down the line it was necessary to go through the whole process in reverse, the train engine coming to a stand at Whaley Bridge's advanced starting signal while the brakes were released. That was not the end of the matter, however, for there was another 1 in 60 descent after Disley requiring first a stop there to apply brakes (AWB in the Working Timetables) and another between Hazel Grove and Woodsmoor level crossing to release them again.

Up trains on this line also stopped at the Bibbington's Sidings starter for brakes to be applied for the 1 in 66 descent into Buxton where they were released while the train was held at No.1's home signal. For some reason the continued application of wagon brakes was considered unnecessary for the short, sharp descent of the Buxton Curve which could sometimes lead to difficulties. On 17 June 1953 Rowsley's Tommy Howarth had an unnerving experience with 90242. He was drawing half a train of loaded limestone wagons out of the Up Sidings prior to picking up the rest when the weight overcame the engine's brakes and away it went down the bank to end up amid the wreckage of the stopblock at East Junction.

The approach from the south on the Ashbourne line with its steep descent from Briggs sidings involved stopping at the box's starting signal or, in the case of trains off the Ladmanlow branch, at Hindlow's starting signal, for brakes to be applied. *Trainmen must satisfy themselves before starting from Hindlow on the down main or from the single line that sufficient hand brakes have been applied* adjured the Sectional Appendix. Release of the brakes was effected on the arches approaching Buxton No.2 signal box.

Despite all these cumbersome hindrances to progress, some six to ten minutes being allowed at each location for the application or release of wagon brakes, there was a healthy and continuous flow of traffic as indicated in the accompanying tables. In the down direction there were ten weekday Midland/Nor'West transfer freights plus seven terminating at Buxton and a further ten starting from Buxton. In the reverse, up, direction there was a slightly different pattern due, it would seem, to a modicum of remarshalling of the empties, five through trains plus thirteen terminating at Buxton and a further eight starting from there. To these must be added three trains in each direction to and from the Sheffield area; some sixty trains in all crawling daily around the countryside.

Then, of course, there were the local trippers and pick-up freights. Target 63, for instance, spent the whole day bustling between the Up and Down Sidings, Midland Yard, Gas Sidings, Ashwood Dale and Higher Buxton; it even managed an evening trip to Briggs Sidings. Movements on the Ashbourne line comprised the trippers in connection with C&HP destinations – Targets 72, 73 and 74 to and from Hindlow/Briggs Sidings and the Ladmanlow branch and Target 76 to and from Friden to connect with a reciprocal service from Middleton – and the through pick-up freights.

DOWN — ASHBOURNE LINE SERVICES (In accordance with freight WTT commencing 5·6·50)

Time at Buxton				
10·30	10·15	Q	G	T73 Engine & brake, Hindlow - Buxton
12/28	10·15		K	T72 Old Harpur - Buxton (Harpur Hill 10·25 - 11·30)
	12/30		K	T73 Mineral, Hindlow - Harpur Hill (Ladmanlow SO)
2/38	2/15		K	T73 Mineral, Hindlow - Buxton
1/45	12/30	SO	J	T76 Mineral, Friden - Buxton
3/15	1/55	SX	J	T76 Mineral, Friden - Hindlow then engine & brake to Buxton
4/32	8-38		K	T81 Freight, Pinfold Sidings - Buxton
6/23	4/50	SO	K	T74 Briggs Sidings - Buxton
7/25	5/30	SX	K	T74 Ladmanlow - Buxton (Hindlow 5/30 - 7/0)
7/38	7/10	SX	K	T63 Mineral, Briggs Sidings - Buxton
8/15	5/35		K	T79 Mineral, Ashbourne - Buxton
8/40	8/15	SO	G	T74 Engine & Brake, Briggs Sdgs - Buxton
8/55	4/44	SX	K	T83 Freight, Pinfold Sidings - Buxton
9/30	7/45	SO	K	T82 Mineral, Hartington - Buxton
10/0	9/40	SO }	G	Engine & brake, Briggs Sdgs - Buxton after working 5/29 SO, 6/46 SX x Stockport
10/10	9/50	SX }		

UP

7·15	SX	K	T72 Buxton - Briggs Sidings - Old Harpur (Assisted Q to Briggs Sdgs. by T66)
7·30	SO	J	T76 Empties, Buxton - Friden assisted by T72 to Briggs Sidings which then goes Mineral to Old Harpur
7·40		J	T73 Empties, Buxton - Hindlow then Q assist T72 to Harpur Hill
8·50	SX	J	T76 Empties, Buxton - Friden
9·10		K	T80 Mineral, Buxton - Dovefields Sidings (Assisted Q to Briggs Sidings)
10·50	Q	K	T73 Mineral, Buxton - Hindlow
1/10	SX }	K	T73 Mineral, {Harpur Hill / Ladmanlow} Hindlow
1/20	SO }		
2/0		K	T79 Mineral, Buxton - Ashbourne
3/0		K	T74 Mineral, Buxton - {Briggs Sdgs. SO / Ladmanlow SX}
4/0	SX	K	T82 Mineral, Buxton - Dovefields Sidings
4/20	SO	K	T82 Mineral, Buxton - Hartington
6/10	SX	K	T63 Mineral, Buxton - Briggs Sidings
7/0	SO	K	T74 Mineral, Buxton - Briggs Sidings
9/0	SO	H	5/29 } Stockport - Briggs Sidings
9/10	SX		6/46 }

Time at Buxton — Q = As required

KM2002

Table showing the quite busy services on the Ashbourne line and Ladmanlow branch – all but the evening train from Stockport being local Target numbers.

A different scene of operations as a returning train of empty Tunstead hoppers, headed by 48711 from Northwich, rattles through Peak Forest having just breasted the summit. These nominal 40 ton (actual 43½) hopper wagons were introduced in 1936 and a total of 165 were put into service. They were eventually given TOPS code PHV and 147 survived until the end of 1997 forming the last regular main line vacuum-braked services in the country. Two of them, the prototype 19000 of 1936 and 19036 of 1938, have been saved for preservation at the Midland Railway Centre. Photograph: E.R. Morten.

These were Target 79 to and from Ashbourne and Targets 80-83 to and from Dovefield Sidings/Pinfold Sidings, both near Uttoxeter, giving a total of ten weekday trains in each direction in and out of Buxton.

Another penalty for being up in the clouds (sometimes literally) was adverse weather conditions, in particular ice and snow. As recounted earlier in BRILL March 1996, 'In the Bleak Midwinter', British Railways had at this time, strategically placed around the system, some 600 steam lances and 550 snowploughs of varying designs. So far as Buxton was concerned, steam lances were located at Buxton Nos.1 and 2 and East Junction signal boxes and, to quote the Sectional Appendix, the equipment comprised *a length of insulated metal tubing with a 15ft to 17ft length of armoured hose and a connection to attach this to the steam tube cleaning cock on the side of the smokebox on standard engines only. It must be understood the non-standard engines have no fitting to accommodate the hose connection. The emission of steam is controlled by the man operating the lance, by means of a trigger on the apparatus after opening the cock on the side of the smokebox.* The purpose of the lances was *to facilitate the clearance of ice and snow from points*, but by whom? *The footplate staff of engines requisitioned for the purpose are responsible for coupling up the apparatus to the locomotive. The steam jet must be directed on to the switches by any Traffic or Permanent Way staff available, who will be responsible for operating the lance, and also for spreading salt after the ice and snow have melted. When using the lance, care must be taken to avoid ballast being lifted by the force of the jet, as there is a possibility of the ballast falling on side chairs and other connections causing subsequent failures.*

At this altitude, however, snow could lay or drift at depths beyond the scope of mere lances to clear and then it was the turn of the ploughs. Buxton had a mixture of

Viewed from the eastern escarpment of Great Rocks Dale, a laden hopper train draws out of the Tunstead Quarry holding sidings – the eponymous Midland signal box is just out of shot to the right. Eight of these trains left daily bound for Hartford or Northwich in connection with the Brunner Mond soda ash plants at Lostock and Winnington. It's worth mentioning that these services still run but these days they comprise a Class 60 diesel at the head of a rake of twenty-five 102 tonne JEA hoppers giving a gross train weight up to 2,455 tonnes. Photograph: E.R. Morten.

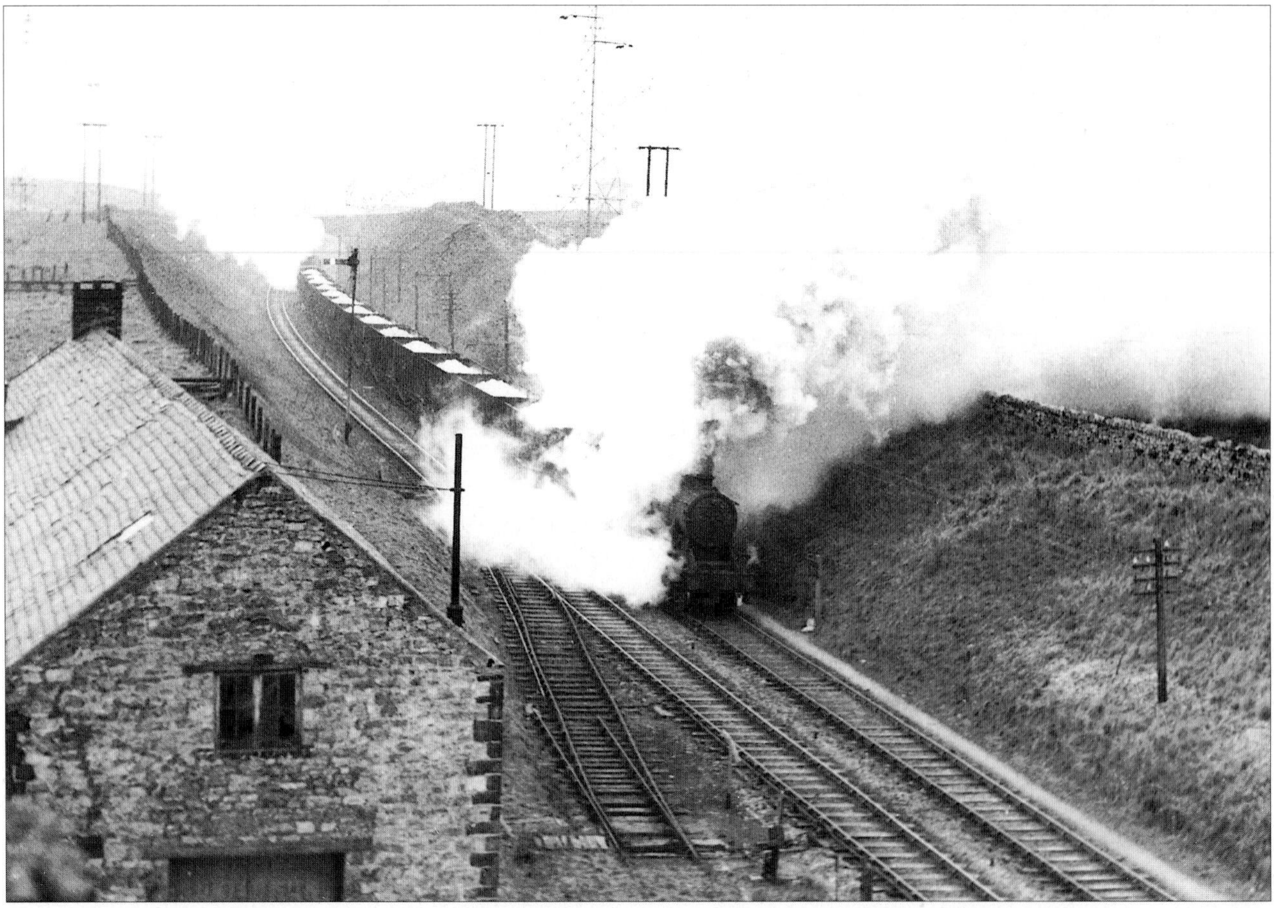

old and new; an old LMS No.3 wood and steel plough for coupling to back-cab Super Ds 49210 or 49348 and a large, all steel, BR No.2 plough for coupling to specially adapted 4F 44339. These usually operated together, coupled back to back, and in case of deep snow, with another engine marshalled in between for extra power. They would patrol the area to keep the lines open, as best they may, to allow the continued movement of traffic.

In those conditions, to mis-quote W.S. Gilbert, a railwayman's lot was not a happy one but, despite all, they turned out to keep the trains running because, as Edgeley driver Jim Howarth put it, *to the old railwayman it was a tradition, it was part of your life – railways went through the back of your spine like Blackpool went through rock!*

Left. **After 8Fs were permanently diagrammed on the hopper trains, about 1938, a turntable was installed next to the Buxton Road bridge at Great Rocks for their sole use. Prior to that they had to go down to the Blackwell triangle, as did all the bankers. Rowsley did, in fact, subsequently acquire a concession for the engine of their 12.15pm class K to use the turntable before returning with the 5.10pm to Rowsley, but that was an exception. Here, in August 1951, Heaton Mersey's 48642 has already turned while another is just leaving the turntable. Photograph: E.R. Morten.**

Below left. **On a dank day in January 1955 a Tunstead hopper train, its limestone gleaming white in the murk, breasts the 1,168ft summit at Bibbington's Sidings. There has been a fall in Dove Holes tunnel and the services have been diverted via Buxton. Since the train is fully fitted (although they all ran under the class D semi-fitted headcode) there's no need to stop to pin down wagon brakes and the train will continue, undeterred, followed by the banker as far as the signal box, just off the picture to the right where it will cross over and retreat back down the hill. Photograph: E.R. Morten.**

Below. **High on a hillside ledge on the line of the old C&HPR, 43296 shunts its train at Harpur Hill. This four mile single track branch to Ladmanlow was more or less on the level, in keeping with its canal-like construction, except for a vicious ascent from its junction with the main Ashbourne line. A 30mph speed limit was imposed over the branch except, as the Sectional Appendix coyly put it, 'over the short length approaching 1 in 41 gradient near Harpur Hill'. The branch was worked by staff and ticket and at Harpur Hill the shunter was authorised to receive or deliver the staff. Between there and Old Harpur, where there was a continuous array of sidings and loops, it was worked as a goods yard. Photograph: E.R. Morten.**

The end of the line! Ladmanlow, 1,266 feet above sea level, where the level crossing gates of Leek Road marked the end of the branch proper; the sidings beyond, where 43268 is standing, were worked as a goods yard. From this point, in the distant past, the original C&HPR plunged down through Burbage Tunnel to Whaley Bridge. The line from Old Harpur to Ladmanlow was closed during the period of this survey in August 1954 and the remainder of the branch was subsequently progressively closed: Harper Hill-Old Harpur February 1966, Hindlow-Harpur Hill September 1973. Photograph: E.R. Morten.

Back to the centre of activity, now in the iron grip of winter, January 1951. Not exactly 'snow up to t'neck' as Charlie Harrison once described it but be sure it was drifting deep into the depressions and cuttings on the tops. 43296 puffs away busily with an Ashbourne line tripper watched by a train crew who are doubtless making their way to No.1 box to relieve a Western Division-bound freight. Photograph: E.R. Morten.

Two glimpses of Buxton's snowplough train at work in February 1955. First the assembly drifts through Hindlow station, 44339 leading with its huge BR No.2 all-steel plough and a Super D carrying its LMS No.3 timber and steel plough at the other end. Marshalled in between is an 8F to give extra oomph! when occasion demands. Behind the train are tank-fed loco watering points, one of only two locations available on the Ashbourne line, the other being at Tissington. The second photograph shows the train attacking drifts at Brigg sidings. In the fields beyond only the tops of the dry stone walls are visible. Photographs: E.R. Morten.

Endpiece

Near the end at Lostock Hall. Photograph Transport Treasury.